"Boyd's vocation to bridge Christian traditions shi[nes...] book. He is a Vineyard pastor who loves Ignatius of Loyola, John Cassian, and Saint Benedict. He is a charismatic who cherishes the contemplative tradition of the church. Somehow in his insightful telling, these diverse streams of the Christian faith fit together harmoniously. This book does a great service to the church by showing charismatics and Pentecostals how the constraint that characterizes monastic practice offers joy, flourishing, and faithfulness."

Tish Harrison Warren, Anglican priest and author of *Liturgy of the Ordinary* and *Prayer in the Night*

"Christianity proposes not so much a set of beliefs as a way of life, a bid for the total transformation and fulfillment of human existence. Jared Boyd, a wise and experienced pastor, unpacks this proposal with insight, fervor, and a gracious sensitivity to contemporary questions and concerns. This book will be for many a welcome challenge and summons to a holistic encounter with God in Christ."

Wesley Hill, associate professor of New Testament at Western Theological Seminary

"The deeply spiritual life is one of release and abandonment, learning how to let go, die to self, and live the abundant life, all within healthy boundaries of love. This is so contrary to the world's way of accumulation, domination, and self-absorption. The ancient fathers and mothers of our faith point us in this direction with humility and grace, and so does Jared Boyd. Reflect deeply and intentionally on the contents herein and watch how your spiritual horizons expand as the freedom of constraint takes root in your soul."

Stephen A. Macchia, founder of Leadership Transformations and director of the Pierce Center at Gordon-Conwell Theological Seminary

"In a world of excess and distraction, constant demands for our attention, and moral confusion, Jared's book is an invaluable resource for the church, not only for those who have a natural leaning toward simplicity and introspection but especially for those who do not. *Finding Freedom in Constraint* is accessible, conversational, and funny. It is filled with wisdom and guidance for incorporating these ancient, life-giving practices into our hearts and our intentionally developed communities. Jared doesn't shy away from engaging the difficult topics in our culture but instead holds them with a gentle, thoughtful, and humble hand that we are wise to emulate."

Jay Pathak, national director of Vineyard USA

"Jared Patrick Boyd has written a beautiful book that enlivened my love for Jesus and made me want to live by greater constraint, a strange but honest statement. But the accessible, tangible way Jared articulates constraint gives vision for the good to run wild. I know this book's author to be a man who has lived his message, who writes not only from his head but even more profoundly from his heart and his bones. If you want a vision for robust, countercultural formation to Jesus—an ancient way in a modern world—look no further than *Finding Freedom in Constraint*."

Tyler Staton, lead pastor at Bridgetown Church and national director of 24-7 Prayer USA

JARED PATRICK BOYD

FINDING

FREEDOM

in CONSTRAINT

*Reimagining Spiritual Disciplines
as a Communal Way of Life*

Foreword by TODD HUNTER

An imprint of InterVarsity Press
Downers Grove, Illinois

FOR JAIME

With you, I have learned to love and be loved.

InterVarsity Press
P.O. Box 1400 | Downers Grove, IL 60515-1426
ivpress.com | email@ivpress.com

©2023 by Jared Patrick Boyd

All rights reserved. No part of this book may be reproduced in any form without written permission from InterVarsity Press.

InterVarsity Press® is the publishing division of InterVarsity Christian Fellowship/USA®. For more information, visit intervarsity.org.

All Scripture quotations, unless otherwise indicated, are taken from The Holy Bible, New International Version®, NIV®. Copyright © 1973, 1978, 1984, 2011 by Biblica, Inc.™ Used by permission of Zondervan. All rights reserved worldwide. www.zondervan.com. The "NIV" and "New International Version" are trademarks registered in the United States Patent and Trademark Office by Biblica, Inc.™

While any stories in this book are true, some names and identifying information may have been changed to protect the privacy of individuals.

The publisher cannot verify the accuracy or functionality of website URLs used in this book beyond the date of publication.

Cover design: David Fassett
Cover images: Getty Images: © 200degrees, © Pakin Songmor
Interior design: Daniel van Loon

ISBN 978-1-5140-0431-9 (print) | ISBN 978-1-5140-0432-6 (digital)

Printed in the United States of America ♾

Library of Congress Cataloging-in-Publication Data
A catalog record for this book is available from the Library of Congress.

30 29 28 27 26 25 24 23 | 13 12 11 10 9 8 7 6 5 4 3 2 1

CONTENTS

FOREWORD

TODD HUNTER

Life is sheer gift. But being alive involves us in a mysterious jumble. We experience our actual lives as grace and goodness intertwined with sinning and being sinned against. Beauty and evil stand together knocking on the doors of our heart and our soul. The bad stuff seems louder, campaigning against our will and emotions with a ferocity that would make even a DC lobbyist blush.

This means that having a life—at least having a meaningful, purposeful life directed at *God's good*—is often a test, occasionally involving painful trials. We know this by experience.

For many of us, the challenge becomes too much. We find ways to retire from "seeking first the kingdom of God." We invent ways to no longer hear Jesus' invitation to "come follow me." We refuse to look across the road, for we might see a Samaritan in need. We learn that it is easier and culturally normative to reject, despise, or condemn an enemy rather than to love him or her, to actively direct our will to seek their good. This is the broad road that leads to destruction.

But another way stands open before us: following the way of Jesus on the narrow path.

The Jesus way requires seeking, within a participative community, a well-ordered life. These are the great insights Jared Boyd brings together in the Order of the Common Life, a missional monastic order. Having done a postulancy cohort led by Jared, I learned some things about the spiritual growth that comes from a community ordered around spiritual transformation into Christlikeness for the sake of being ambassadors of God's kingdom, agents of his healing and redemptive love.

Thankfully with the publishing of *Finding Freedom in Constraint,* you can get both insight into and a taste of the possibilities of a well-ordered life. But be prepared for surprising revelations, for counterintuitive insights along the ancient and sacred path to spirituality in the way of Jesus.

In my postulancy cohort, I was given an environment in which I deepened my ability to notice the love of God and to nurture receptivity to it. I was given the gift of space to reimagine my vocation to follow Jesus for the sake of others. I learned, again, that information and content alone are not transformative, that engaging my will and engaging with a community are vital to real, lasting transformation. I discerned where I felt trapped by an over-full life and discovered an appropriate rhythm of life for someone in their late sixties. I could go on for pages with highlights from my journal.

The power of good questions. The gift of being listened to. The sense of the presence of God. All of this, even when striving to look deeply within, was hopeful and pleasant. It was not a legalistic grind or religious chore. Rather, I found myself being organically more peacefully present to life.

Over our months together as a cohort I found myself wishing that others could experience this too. With the publication of this book, now you can receive an orientation to what a well-ordered life in a community seeking transformation looks and feels like.

Jared is wise. He knows, as Jesus taught, that wheat and weeds grow in the world until the final judgment, and that Jesus is superintending this reality. For our purposes in this book, it is crucial to note that weeds do not just grow in the world outside us, they grow with the good wheat in our hearts and souls too.

This can be frightening. It can lead to lots of harmful self-talk, to dysfunctional feelings of guilt, or worse, to sibilating shame. I want to ask you to trust that God knows what he is doing in your life, just as he knows what is happening in the world. Don't try to get ahead of God, don't try to hurry the pace of transformation. God is patient with weeds that remain. Just gently and peacefully keep seeking first Jesus and the kingdom of God.

As you begin to turn the pages to hear Jared's voice, I want you to relax. A well-ordered life that others experience as for their good awaits you as you practice what Jared teaches: the intelligent, grace-based practices of ancient and anointed Christian spirituality.

INTRODUCTION

The goal of Christian spiritual formation is to learn to experience the love of God and to learn to love as God loves. This is the simplest way I know to explain the spiritual journey. But what stands in the way of this journey is often unseen. And what is unseen has formidable strength to keep us in bondage to the things that prevent us from experiencing the love of God and from loving others in the way that God loves them.

The experience of the love of God is at the center of this book.

The love of God is the only thing that empowers real change in our lives.

God is always present to us. And we are often not present to God. We are caught up in an array of distractions, pursuits, and thoughts that draw us away from the experience of God's love.

An important process in the spiritual formation journey—one that can help free us from the things that keep us bound—is getting a clear view of what prevents us from loving and being loved.

What is in the way? What prevents me from living into all that God is inviting me toward and saying yes to every invitation that God extends?

The answer to this question is different for each person. As Roberta Bondi articulates, "What prevents me from loving may be entirely different than what prevents you from loving."[1]

But getting a clear view of the things that disrupt our formation is becoming more difficult. We've lost some things along the way that the earliest generations of Christ-followers placed at the center of their way of life. The pursuit of *humility*, for starters.

This book is a vision for engaging and reimagining the way of life that emerged in those early years. It is meant to allow the way of life early Christians pursued to address the current crises of discipleship. But this isn't early-church nostalgia. It's a vision for reimagining a *way of life* that has bolstered the formation of the Christian person in the way of love since the very beginning.

Our culture increasingly obscures our view of what keeps us in bondage. It is easy for us to grow accustomed to the very things that hold us back from a life devoted to being united to God. Our culture is perfectly designed to keep us distracted, disembodied, and removed from our own *self*.

We often live in invisible chains, which cause us to settle for a vision of our life that is so much less than the vision offered by God in Christ, who is nonetheless kind and loving and gentle and patient with us.

Some of these invisible chains are built for us by giant computers whose primary job is to learn how to keep our attention on the small black mirror we hold in our hands. The feed on that screen reflects our own desires.

We make other chains all on our own. The first step toward freedom is the willingness to embrace the reality that this is the state of things: there are things hidden from our view that get in the way of what we really want.

We should not be afraid or ashamed of this fact. It's just *true*.

But neither should we ignore it.

Many of us live with the assumption that whatever is in the way of a better life—and in the case before us, a better *spiritual* life—resides outside of us. When we consider why we are not growing spiritually or growing more in our love for God and neighbor—which sums up the whole spiritual journey as described by Jesus—we often assume it has to do with something external to us.

We change churches. We find new podcasts. We buy a new book (this one included). We search for some external thing that will give us what we're looking for. A conference. A new method. New spiritual practices and workouts. The changes we often seek in order to bolster our spiritual life are primarily external. But the things that keep us bound up and stuck are not external to us. They are within us.

This is what all good spiritual guides have taught us. And it is within the tradition that gave us these guides that I offer this book. The things that bind us can only do so to the extent that they remain hidden to us. But once we see them clearly—those inner masters that rule us and rob us of our freedom—we can join Christ, who is already present doing the slow work of healing us.

This is not a self-help book. It's an invitation to see the way the love of God is the only thing, in the end, that does the work of transformation.

Addressing the things that hinder our spiritual freedom—the shame, the patterns of personality, the habits that keep us stuck, and the stories we tell about ourselves and others—is becoming easier and more accessible as social scientists and psychologists continue to give us data.

Tools and books for spiritual formation are now ubiquitous in the twenty-first-century Western church. Even in church communities where two decades ago any talk of spiritual formation, contemplation, and spiritual direction were met with great caution ("Aren't these New Age practices?"), you can now find Enneagram workshops, classes on centering prayer, and even a cadre of pew-sitters who have discovered the *Spiritual Exercises* of Saint Ignatius of Loyola. Brené Brown's war on shame is becoming household language,[2] and others are building on that work.[3] Having a therapist, being in a twelve-step recovery program, or pursuing marriage counseling is no longer met with suspicion from the church. The church, it seems, is growing in her capacity to care for souls.

The *way of life* that I'm inviting you toward is to live in such a way that those unseen things will quite regularly rise to the surface. What is now hidden will be revealed. And the church and the Spirit will guide you toward your freedom, which is your inheritance in Christ.

With all this talk about freedom, perhaps you are wondering how and why this book is also about *constraint?*

A Way of Life

In the span of about a hundred years, in the middle of the desert of modern-day Turkey and the mountain region outside of Alexandria, Egypt, a peculiar *way of life* emerged in the late third and early fourth century as a countercultural movement. A man named Athanasius was doing important theological work on the heels of the Council of Nicaea, one of the most important church meetings of all time. He also wrote a "bestseller"—the *Life of Anthony*, a biography of a peculiar man who spent most of a twenty-year span living alone in a desert. His quiet life of constraint catalyzed a generation of early Christian practice.

This biography of Anthony spread an understanding of this way of life, which was growing at a steady pace and would soon be codified, organized, and shared. The church had already been undergoing a dramatic (and perhaps unfortunate) shift with the conversion of the Roman Emperor Constantine, making Christianity a state-sponsored religion. But outside the seats of power and influence were an increasing number of men and women who quietly shaped the future of Christian spirituality and discipleship. This *way of life* captured the attention of Saint Augustine, Saint Basil of Caesarea, Saint Macrina the Younger, and to some extent Basil's younger brother Gregory of Nyssa.

These are the ones whose books and stories you might know. They wrote the historical record and crafted history with their very lives. But countless men and women who had no title or position, many of whom you may have never heard—Pachomius, Saint Scholastica, Evagrius—created Christian community and spiritual formation practices that made the lives of the men and women we read about, and their contribution to the church, possible.

This *way of life* centered around practices of constraint. It marked out specific rhythms of prayer and work and study. It eventually gave birth to monasticism—men and women living in communities with a shared set of practices—and it became the primary model of intentional spiritual formation for most of the next thirteen hundred years.

As this *way of life* became institutionalized in those first few centuries, it would radically transform culture. It would inspire men like Benedict of Nursia, who founded the Benedictine communities, which were refined by later generations, who planted Cistercian monasteries like the Abbey of Gethsemani, where Thomas Merton lived and wrote and reimagined what the life of a monk could become.

Mother Teresa also followed in this tradition and way of life, founding her own religious order—the Missionaries of Charity— in 1950 with a singular focus on serving the poor in Calcutta, India.

Saint Francis of Assisi, Saint Ignatius of Loyola, Saint Teresa of Ávila, and Saint John of the Cross all lived and prayed and served the church tethered to a *way of life* rooted in constraint. More recently Thomas Keating, André Louf, and Frs. Richard Rohr, Ronald Rolheiser, and Basil Pennington have lived and prayed and served the church in this way of life. There are countless brothers and sisters who have kept this spiritual tradition alive, many living quietly enough to go unnoticed but faithful enough to be a ballast in the ship of the church since before our creeds were established.

There have always been men and women who have held and lived this wisdom of constraint, and they have been one of the most overlooked cultural forces in history. You have probably thought little about them. This book is an invitation to move your life toward their way of life—a life of constraint. It is an invitation to the deep formation that is possible when a life of constraint is embraced in community.

A life with some constraints makes a life of freedom possible.

A Rule of Life

The pursuit of freedom through the practice of constraint is a well-worn path. What began in the desert with men like Saint Anthony living alone in caves morphed into men and women practicing the way of constraint together in community. Small communities formed around shared practices, at first out of the simple need to survive. It turns out that being completely alone is much harder than people imagine. Simple practicalities of survival drew these men and women together into shared housing, shared rhythms of prayer and work, and shared resources. This allowed the pursuit of this way of life to flourish in ways that it could not when practiced alone.

Sharing this way of life with others had a multiplying effect. There was more time for prayer when you were not the only one thinking about the food you would eat tomorrow. Within a few short decades the so-called ideal ascetic life of a holy man living in a cave was more or less abandoned. Community and shared common life were the future, even if shorter periods of cave and desert dwelling were permissible.

From these new communities emerged a peculiar form of literature as the monastic "rule of life" took shape.[4] It turns out that it isn't only the case where two or three are gathered together— "there the Lord is." It turns out that where two or three are gathered together—there also is a great need to write some things down that those two or three can agree upon. Somebody needs to do the dishes.

So already constraint begins its work because agreeing with two or three others on how you should live your life together is an excellent lesson in constraint. There can be no community without particular constraints. Marriage, for example, is the constraint of a certain kind of love to one other person; a family is constrained by both spoken and unspoken rules that govern a household; the people of God are constrained, as the apostle Paul notes, by the love of Christ (2 Cor 5:14).

Community requires constraint.

By the time Saint Benedict came around in the late fifth century, there were several rule-of-life documents representing various approaches, all of which were trying to give shape to both individual and communal life. By the ninth century, more than twenty-five rules of life existed. Saint Benedict's Rule became the most influential throughout monastic communities, even though most of it was borrowed and liberally modified from a rule known as the Rule of the Master. It was in use well before Benedict arrived on the scene. As Esther de Waal points out, Benedict

> was happy to take what was good from the existing monastic heritage, to make it his own, and to colour it with his own personal experience. As he looked round he found various types of monastic life with their own traditions and achievements. There were some forms of life which allowed much scope for individual development and for the life of solitude; others stressed more the value of a corporate life in a settled community. He drew these different strands together.[5]

Something Is Missing in Our Formational Practices

In the preface to *The Spirit of the Disciplines,* Dallas Willard lays before us two tasks that are vital if Christianity is to be a guide for humanity:

> First, it must take the need for human transformation as seriously as do modern revolutionary movements. The modern negative critique of Christianity arose in the first place because the church was not faithful to its own message—it failed to take human transformation seriously as a real, practical issue to be dealt with in realistic terms.

Second, it needs to clarify and exemplify realistic methods of human transformation. It must show how the ordinary individuals who make up the human race can become, through the grace of Christ, a love-filled, effective, and powerful community.[6]

I miss Dallas Willard.

He goes on to articulate his vision for the second task, masterfully painting the contours of the spiritual life and demonstrating how our body—that's right, our *body*—is a "primary *resource* for the spiritual life."[7] He writes what has become a classic work on the spiritual disciplines in support of his central claim that we in fact *can* become like Christ by following him in his lifestyle, which includes "solitude and silence, prayer, simple and sacrificial living, intense study and meditation on God's Word and God's ways, and service to others."[8]

It would be hard to improve on Willard's articulation of the spiritual disciplines. And when we combine Willard's insights with Richard Foster's *Celebration of Discipline*, which was published a decade earlier, it seems we have what we need to begin practicing the spiritual disciplines in a way that leads to deeper formation and transformation. Those two books have done tremendous work in guiding people into a new way of living.

Yet nearly everyone who tries on a life of practicing the spiritual disciplines learns quickly that formational practices are difficult to stick to. Practicing forms of spiritual life that require discipline is really hard. We are often missing a key component that I think can make our practices stick. It's also the primary component of the monastic tradition—the tradition that both Willard and Foster and many others are drawing from. It's the monastic tradition that has kept this way of life and the practices of spiritual disciplines alive when, as Willard himself concedes, the practice of the disciplines became for all practical purposes lost to us in Western Christianity. I think we need to take up Willard's first task. We "must take the need for human transformation as seriously as do modern revolutionary movements."

The problem with leaning into a life of *constraint*, which is the primary way I will be talking about the spiritual disciplines, is that we almost exclusively have tried to do it alone. We have few living models for what it looks like to do it together. This is an unfortunate and unforeseen consequence of the Reformation, which systematically threw out the "baby" of the religious life of monks and nuns along with the "bathwater" that the Reformers wanted to throw out—however you want to describe that bathwater. What was lost in the Reformation (for those of us who are not Catholic or Orthodox) was the institution of monastic communities bearing witness to a communal way of life that centered on the practice of constraint.

Willard and Foster, and others such as David Benner, Ruth Haley Barton, and Kathleen Norris, have drunk deeply from the life that the monastic tradition has brought us. They've gifted us with writing about the riches they themselves have gleaned in conversations with abbots and sisters at retreats in monasteries and convents. But the key component that has been left out in most of our attempts to lean into these practices is a commitment to doing so alongside others in a vulnerable way.

Call it spiritual companionship.

Call it spiritual friendship.

Call it monastic.

But the spiritual disciplines were never meant to be primarily practiced alone. We are meant to share the joys and burdens of the practice of spiritual disciplines with others. The formation that comes from practicing constraint happens mostly when we practice alongside others.

This book is an invitation to practice constraint in community.

Over the past ten years, I have been slowly trying to reimagine the tradition that has carried the communal practice of constraint in monasteries and religious orders. I believe that monasticism and religious orders as institutions of the church will have a resurgence in the days ahead. The result of that reimagining work, and my own contribution to that hoped-for future, is the Order of the Common Life—an ecumenical religious order for the twenty-first century.[9] Since the middle of the twentieth century there have been several men and women living in monastic communities or as part of a traditional Catholic religious order who have made it clear that, unless this tradition is reimagined and rearticulated, it will die. Thomas Merton spent much of his own monastic vocation thinking and writing about what is at the core of this tradition. Merton himself wondered how we might authentically carry it—reimagine it—for the sake of the church.

I've committed the rest of my life to the same question that Merton was asking: How do we authentically continue this tradition? We have invited men and women from around the world to consider and discern whether or not they have what has been traditionally referred to as a *religious vocation*. We lead people through a multi-year discernment process around our own rule of life. Our primary *charism* (gift) that we offer the world is the work of helping people notice and nurture the work of God in their lives and in the lives of others. We believe that the most important human experience is the experience of the love of God. You can explore more about our dispersed community and read our rule of life at www.orderofthecommonlife.org.

The six commitments of constraint in the second half of this book are drawn from our last decade of trying to work this out with others. And, while these commitments alone do not constitute a rule of life, they offer an introduction to a way of life for you and your community, church, or family. If these practices resonate with you, I invite you to consider wading in a little deeper through our dispersed community of the Order of the Common Life.

An Overview

In this book, I offer three meditations, a practical overview, six practices of constraint meant to be done in community, and a very short invitation. I have just one hope for you: that you can begin a journey of finding freedom through the practice of constraint, sustained by the presence of others who are on the journey with you.

This book centers around the practice of constraint, but at the center of it all is the ability to see a greater degree of the love of God. Most of us are not actively looking for ways for our life to be constrained. When I first mentioned this project to a friend and got to the part about challenging people to take on some constraint, his honest response was "That sounds terrible." I offer a vision of why we need constraint, and I hope that you will welcome more constraint than you ever thought possible.

Freedom is a theme that we're all aware of, particularly for those living in America. And yet the freedom I'm advocating for is entirely different from the freedom we hear about in our cultural context. The freedom that the best guides of the contemplative tradition talk about has little to do with getting what you want. In fact, it has more to do with not getting what you want than it has to do with almost anything else.

In parts two and three, I offer six practices of constraint. I could have chosen others, of course. These six shouldn't necessarily have priority over other practices—with the exception of silence and solitude, which is foundational to any contemplative work. I don't believe any real discipleship can happen apart from the practice of silence and solitude. It's why these practices show up in nearly every book on spiritual disciplines. I'll offer some basic guidance for practicing the practices, but I'm more interested in helping us understand *why* silence and solitude do so much heavy lifting in the contemplative and formational stream. We learn silence and solitude through practice. My goal is to help us desire the gift that they can bring.

If you find yourself struggling to work through some of these constraints, you are in good company. I have a lot of hope for the church to lean in this direction, but it is a hope tempered by reality. I have been trying to live a way of life with some constraints at the center for nearly a decade. There has been a lot of ego and fear and a host of things that have needed to receive the healing love of God in my life as I have leaned into some of these practices. The way of life that I'm inviting you into is full of struggle. But the struggle is actually part of the work. We have rarely created spaces to talk about the struggle of these practices; I'm trying to change that.

Finally, this book is meant to be a guide for communities of formation, primarily as a resource in the local church, for ordinary people like you and me, living ordinary lives, learning how to love through practicing together a way of life in community, sharing commitments to practices that will deepen our capacity to love one another.

As you work your way through this book in community, I hope what begins to surface is a vision for how this *way of life* might be lived together within your local church. I've created additional resources for you that can be accessed at www.jaredpatrickboyd.com.

For now, I invite you to notice and nurture the work that God does in you while you read this book. Discuss it with others. Try on some practices. Keep a journal. Set aside time to pray.

But please do not read this book alone.

This book is meant to be discussed and its practices are meant to be practiced alongside others. Visit www.orderofthecommonlife.org for guidance on how to form a conversation group around this book in your local church or join a group online. There will be plenty of opportunities to do this work together.

But don't be a hermit in a cave.

Part One

THE
SHAPE
OF
CONSTRAINT

CHAPTER ONE

RIVER, the WOMB, and HEARTH

A MEDITATION ON THE CONSTRAINTS OF THE CHURCH

Some tear away from her and attack her and break her
established rules. They abandon the maternal womb
and the sweet nourishment of the church.

HILDEGARD VON BINGEN,
DOCTOR OF THE UNIVERSAL CHURCH

The church in America is having a moment. Some of our difficulties have been made more poignant by the Covid-19 pandemic, political divisions, and the emergence of #ChurchToo stories of sexual abuse and cover up. We are in the middle of a reckoning. But none of the challenges the church has seen in the past few years are the cause of the reckoning.

The things in our life that we cannot see have great power. Sometimes we get a look at what lies beneath slowly over time through practices of paying deeper attention, and sometimes it just surfaces all at once. The church in America is having an all-at-once moment. We are clearly learning that our way of life—our way of being the church—has not produced the kind of Jesus-followers we have hoped for. Even some who were tasked with leading, pastoring, and caring for us have proven unreliable.

My prayer for the church is that this moment be more than a reckoning. Perhaps it could be another Reformation. But first we have to be honest about what is actually happening. We have to deal with reality.

We are living through a moment when many are deconstructing their Christian faith and abandoning, as Hildegard von Bingen called it, "the maternal womb and the sweet nourishment of the church."[1] I can't necessarily fault them. The carnage and misunderstanding around the so-called deconstruction project only illustrates the point that has led to so many people walking away from church: it has not been a safe place for those who have questions about doctrine, anger about cover ups, and little hope that we will ever be able to detox from the power, money, and exploitation that is woven into the fabric of the church in America.

As I write, I wonder how a book on constraint and spiritual practices could begin to be helpful, given how much of the deconstruction conversation centers around the unhelpful (to some) and unhealthy (real or perceived) constraints and rigidity of certain pockets of the church.

I have hope and a vision for a church that leans into spiritual practices in healthy ways—ways that invite people into deeper commitment. We can learn how to invite people into deeper practice without exerting power over them.

But first we need to bind up some wounds.

This chapter is both for those who love the church and for those leaving it. Most particularly, it is for those who think that by leaving the church they are loving it more. I believe we are living in a moment of reformation. This is my invitation for you to stay in the church—perhaps in some creative ways. It's also meant to be a pushback on church leaders who are dismissive of those wanting to leave it.

If you are wondering if a metaphor can save your faith (or maybe your faith in the church)—I have three of them that I think could, at the very least, be helpful.

The Church as River—and the Banks of Deconstruction

There is a river in Peru that you have probably never heard of. It's the main headstream of the Amazon River, which you certainly have heard of. The Ucayali River has received some attention recently from geologists because we are now able to see how the surface of the earth is changing and how those changes—in vegetation, glacial melting, and even the emergence of new cities—impact the flow of rivers. The shape of the Ucayali River is changing at an impressive speed and through thirty years of satellite images, scientists are able to visualize and predict those changes and look closer at the "meander migration rate" of the river whose waters eventually flow into the Amazon.[2]

The banks of the river give way to its surroundings and the river spills out and forms new bends and necks and chutes. The flow of the river in general is *constrained* by the banks of the river, and the banks of the river respond to the surrounding changes. And yet the river never stops flowing. Some new bends disappear and dry up. Some old banks get eroded. But the direction of the river does not change. The waters end up flowing more or less along the same path.

The church is a river that started as a small stream, birthed by the Spirit, on the day of Pentecost. We are meant to be, as the psalmist says, "a river whose streams make glad the city of God" (Ps 46:4). We are meant to be the place where the presence of God dwells. We carry the water of life, which is the Holy Spirit, and that water nourishes trees of life, which bear all kinds of fruit. The leaves of those trees are for the healing of the nations (Rev 22:2). This is the glorious vision given to us in the revelation of John and, long before him, through a vision in Ezekiel (Ezek 47)—a vision of water spilling out of the temple (which we now know to be both the body of Christ and his church), flowing under the threshold and expanding into the whole world, where every living creature who comes in contact with it will have life abundant.

But what happens when the banks of the river begin to collapse due to weakness? Or the waters of the river become so strong that they spill out and begin to bend the river in a new direction? You might fear that the banks of the river—the strong constraints of the church—are crumbling. People are asking questions about long-held doctrines and teachings of the church and many others are walking through a process of deconstruction. Few pastors know what to do with it all. The once-sturdy banks that held the water of faith for many are shifting in some places. And the questions people are asking and the conclusions they are coming to feel incongruent with the story as it has been told thus far. Theologians and laypeople alike are standing in the waters of the river, which seem to be cresting the banks and overflowing the constraints the church has provided.

Maybe you are looking for ways for the banks to be reshaped so the water can overflow them. Perhaps you see something on the horizon that others are unable to see. You have prayerfully reached conclusions that make others uncomfortable, and you wonder if the church can hold space for the questions you are asking and the tentative conclusions you are reaching. You hold big questions about last things and eternal places. You wonder how the death of Christ brings salvation and healing. And you have questions about human sexuality and the authority of Scripture—and how to think about these in relation to your queer friends and gay neighbors. You might feel frustrated by the slowness of change. You've probably thought about leaving the church. Or perhaps you have already done so.

This moment is one of incredible tension. The river is rushing, the rapids are churning, and we are either headed for a giant flood or damming barrier or bifurcation. The tension is between strict and sturdy banks and the waters that overflow them (as they sometimes should). But this is not a new phenomenon within the church. This is what the church has always been. It has always been a river whose banks are being defined and redefined in an ongoing process of discernment. At our best, we have done this alongside the Spirit, interpreting the Scriptures, living in and responding to the world around us, while loving one another. At our worst, we have done it with a tremendous exertion of power over people.

However the future unfolds, I pray that we not exert power over one another during this season of deconstruction and reformation. If you are a church leader or pastor, I invite you to consider a constraint on your exertion of power over others.

The Early Years

When we think about the early years of the church, we often sigh with relief when we come to the first ecumenical council at Nicaea, where the sturdy banks of the river began to be formed. The Nicene Creed, which eventually provided a benchmark for orthodoxy, was the primary artifact that emerged from the council. In it we find a sense of settledness around important doctrines that we now simply take for granted.

What we often overlook is that coming to some final conclusions around some of the words that would make it into the creed was quite tumultuous for the church. There were some "conservatives" who did not want to accept the wording about Jesus being "one in being with the Father." It took another 350 years for the turbulent waters of the river to settle and the doctrinal banks of the river to stabilize. For much of the fifth, sixth, and seventh centuries, the battles over the nature of Christ—his humanity, his divinity, and how those two could be held together in one body—splintered the church. The waters sometimes overflowed the banks. And sometimes they receded. Friendships were lost, men were murdered, and emperors were conscripted into doctrinal battles.

Maximus the Confessor lived most of his life as a monk in prayer, study, and constraint. He became connected with the theological traditions that informed those early formulations of the nature of Christ that we find in those first creeds. This issue was highly significant for the early church fathers, and it became important for Maximus, who courageously inserted himself into the debate when it became clear that the majority view was not aligned with what was penned at that first council and ratified at the second. Whatever sturdy banks existed at the end of the fourth century were on the verge of collapse. Maximus could not remain silent, so around the year 640, he began to speak out against a popular view that was held by the majority of those in power. He did so in a time when speaking out against those with ecclesial and political power could get you "canceled" in ways that we can't even begin to understand. People were sent to islands to die for not conforming.

For nearly fifteen years Maximus quietly opposed some of the theological changes that were making the rounds. He argued for a return to orthodoxy as established by the first and second ecumenical councils. Whatever this new bend in the river was, for Maximus it was taking the whole river in a dangerous direction. In 655 he was arrested, brought to trial for treason, and accused of heresy. Every attempt to persuade Maximus of the truth of the "emerging view" failed. He was brought to Constantinople where he was tortured for his "heresy." They cut out his tongue to prevent him from speaking, and they cut off his right hand so that he could not write to defend his position. He was exiled to a distant place where he died nearly a decade later with two disciples by his side. Within twenty years of his death, the teaching for which he had given his life was vindicated at the sixth ecumenical council. The "majority opinion" in Maximus's world turned out to be wrong.

Where do we fit into this story? It's a good question for us to think about, particularly if we find ourselves in the midst of chipping away at the banks of the river on the one hand, or trying to keep the water at bay on the other. This analogy of the church as a river, moving in a particular direction, whose banks and boundaries are in flux gives us at least two things to consider as we move forward.

First, some riverbanks are negotiable, and the church's task is ongoing discernment. Discernment of the Scriptures keeps the river flowing, and this has always been done as a collective people in ongoing presence to one another and love for one another. This process is often slow, and we can allow this slow process to constrain us.

Sometimes the banks of the river are held in place by the institution of the church. And sometimes that same institutional structure keeps a bank intact that later generations find unnecessary. We live in the church, and the church is a place of contradiction because, for example, in some parts women can preach and in other parts they are not allowed to preach. From early on the church has convened councils, appointed leaders, commissioned preachers, discerned theological necessities, and drawn boundaries in various places. All have shaped the flow of the river.

Sometimes we look back at earlier decisions and see where the church has made adjustments. We widen the banks in places and counteract erosion in others. Sometimes we can see more clearly than those who came before us, and sometimes our vision has become less clear and we must return to the foundation that has come before us. Navigating this process has always been one of the tasks of the church. This has happened in areas of theology (have you recently met a Monophysite?), worship (the iconoclast debate raged for centuries), and even social and ethical teachings (the first church institution to give a thumbs up to any form of contraception was the Anglican Church in 1930). The church has been at the task of negotiation and discernment from the very beginning.

What we need is patience.

But we also sometimes need impatience. Yes, there are places in this negotiation process where we need to allow things to unfold slowly. But there are other places where we need voices (particularly ones that have been suppressed) to speak loudly and disruptively and to cause conflict.

We find ourselves in a moment where there is a great temptation to hang on to power (if we have it) or exercise the only last freedom we believe we have (if we don't have power)—which is the freedom to leave. The gift of constraint is that we can both constrain our power (if we have it) and allow ourselves to be constrained by the church (if we do not have the power to change it) so that when the time is right, we are still in the river when it shifts in the direction guided by the Spirit.

We can learn to relinquish that particular kind of power that can become toxic and controlling. We can make more room for the marginalized voices of those who can see what others may not yet be able to see. We can stay in the river and do the hard work of confrontation. I'm inspired by the many people who are doing this while not giving up on the church.

This does not mean that anyone should stay in a section of the river that has become toxic. There are traditions and teachings within the church that are harmful and will soon dry up. There are systems and leaders that are toxic. If this is where you are, find a boat and row for fresher waters. If you want to row out of the boundaries of a particular denominational structure, this doesn't mean you have to leave the broader constraints of the historic church. The river is wide and is fed by fresh springs in so many places. Find a church that you can heal in, but please stay in the waters.

Second, the negotiation process goes better with humility— both in those who want to keep everything the same and those who want to bend the banks in a particular direction.

So many of the issues we face today over contentious topics are difficult to talk about without producing a dumpster fire on Twitter. Issues of human sexuality and identity, the role of women in the church and feminism, critical race theory and racial justice, to name just a few, are not going away—we will continue to need to navigate these issues. I hope this process is one where we do not cut out tongues and chop off hands. We have our own culturally bound ways of succumbing to this behavior. This doesn't mean that we can't say what we think and draw boundaries and artic-ulate how we read the Scriptures, but I hope we can do so with a greater degree of humility.

The constraints of the church—the historic creeds, the tradi-tions of reading the Scriptures, care for the poor, and the shared commitment to the praise of God—provide basic boundaries for the river of God's unending love to flow into the world. It's a mess of a river right now, but stay in it—part of that mess may help us grow into what we were always intended to be.

The Church as Womb

There are a lot of metaphors in Scripture for the work of the church. One of the earliest is the church as mother and ourselves as preborn babies. We are within the church's womb being formed into what we were always meant to become—human beings.

I learned of this metaphor in a graduate course with Orthodox theologian Fr. John Behr. It has nudged me toward an imaginative framework where I can, at least in a thought experiment, begin with the possibility that I am not yet a human but am on my way toward becoming one through the nourishment of the church. The most beautiful thing about this image, as Fr. Behr points out, is that we are the recipients of care and nourishment.

So much of our talk about following Jesus is framed in terms of *mission*. We are enfolded into a great family spread across time and place, and we have a job to do. The family business is mission. This, of course, is all true. The church is joining God on mission to the world, which is why we often gravitate to sermons and books that help teach us how to enact our faith outwardly and join God on God's mission.

But the vision of the church as a mother helps us grow deeper into the reality that the totality of our Christian experience is not focused on accomplishing a task. What we often overlook in our pursuit of the mission is that something is happening *to* us. And this work of formation is ongoing until we are born again at our death, in resurrection, when the fullness of time and maturation is complete. We typically think of ourselves as already being human; being "born again" happens at baptism when we receive the Holy Spirit. But let's consider that everything that is happening in our life and all the ways we are learning to love and forgive, rejoice and grieve, hold on to and let go of, are happening within the womb. The church is our mother.[3]

Spiritual formation is not a solo expedition. It is primarily communal. The people of the church are the womb of our formation. And, of course, when those people gather together, leadership is required, and so we have people *and* an institution.

This is where the tension emerges between exercising one's individual freedom and renouncing some of that individual freedom for the sake of the whole. When we entrust leadership to pastors and leaders and overseers, we are handing over some level of authority to the church as our mother. Many modern Americans will hate this choice and try to find a way around it simply because we've been led to believe that freedom is equal to the absence of constraints.

There is no way around this tension. Community is not possible for people who are first and foremost committed to living without constraint. The only way community is possible is for people to negotiate a healthy relinquishment of some things for the sake of other things that serve the whole community. A failure to live in this tension is the primary reason that American evangelicalism feels like it might be collapsing.

I'm offering a different vision of freedom. It is the freedom found *within* the constraints. The scary thing about community and institutions that provide concrete actions for the people within community is that leaders must also be committed to the constraints of leadership. And when we aren't committed to the constraints of the pastoral vocation, we end up with a variety of abuses. Leaders are meant to serve those they are leading, which sometimes means asking people to do things that they do not really (at first) want to do. But leaders also bear the responsibility of shaping a community as a womb—not as a gauntlet.

This is not necessarily a book about leadership. But there are practices here that will make you a better leader as you bring others into your life in an intimate way to practice together. I believe if you do so, it will help make your church into a womb where people can grow.

The church is often pushing people out of the womb who don't quite carry the exact DNA that they or we are looking for. We need to create a more spacious room because the people we push out probably have a lot to teach us. I am not advocating for throwing out orthodoxy for the sake of accommodation. But we need more space for people who are asking hard questions and going through deconstruction.

If you are one of those people who feel pushed out too soon, I'm sorry. I want you to have a womb where you can be formed in the way of Jesus.

Recently a friend in a small Midwestern city told me that for nearly three years they have been looking for a church that believes in the resurrection, prays for the sick, cares for the poor (including refugees), and isn't hitched to the wagon of Christian nationalism. They simply cannot find a church in their city that is passionate enough about the things of Jesus and dispassionate enough about who is going to be the next president. I talk with people all across the country who share this same story. We're in a historic moment that will require a new way of staying in the river—which is actually quite old. We will need to build some new structures and institutions that nurture our formation within the womb of the church.

The Church as a Hearth: That I Might Become "All Flame"

There's a story in *The Sayings of the Desert Fathers* that goes like this:

> Abba Lot went to Abba Joseph and said to him, "Abba, as far as I can I say my little office, I fast a little, I pray and meditate, I live in peace and as far as I can, I purify my thoughts. What else can I do?" Then the old man stood up and stretched his hands towards heaven. His fingers became like ten lamps of fire and he said to him, "If you will, you can become all flame."[4]

When I was sixteen years old, I came into a Vineyard church from a nearby Nazarene church that was a womb to me at the beginning of my faith. I came to Christ in that Nazarene church, with a gospel presentation and an altar call.

My conversion was a moment. I was twelve or thirteen years old. I felt the weight of God come upon me, was filled with the Holy Spirit, and fell to my knees and wept uncontrollably at the grace of God. I needed it more than I needed anything. Even as I write this I am filled with tears of gratitude. I cannot tell this story without weeping because whatever began in me that day has been a relentless healing of wounds and an ongoing invitation to be filled up with the love of God.

I know that not every conversion story is this dramatic. But mine was.

So when I walked into a Vineyard church as a teenager a few years later, whatever I had experienced in my conversion—that overwhelming sense of God's love for me—by this time was more or less a distant memory. It was the worship that got me. I opened up my hands and turned them upward near my waist, and God filled those hands with his love and then dumped the rest of it on top of me, and I began to weep again, standing in the love of God. Something new was birthed within the global church in those years. And this new style of worship that was being nurtured in and through the Vineyard movement seemed to be somewhere near the center of it. At least it was for me.

In different seasons—though not in every season, as I've been through my own radical deconstruction/reconstruction—I have felt as though God's own self was on fire inside of me. If the church had not guided me into the tradition and given me an array of perspectives on the Scriptures, teaching me to read and meditate on the story handed down to us, the deconstruction I faced in the spring of 2002 would likely have burned up my life.

"All flame" means to allow the love of God to consume all that is not of God and to burn and to give off heat and light and draw the world toward the love of God with one's life. But, in order to burn this hot, we need a hearth.

This last metaphor that I offer is the idea that we are meant to burn with the fire of God's very own being, and that the church, at her best, will help that fire burn as hot as possible. If you have ever warmed yourself in front of a fire in someone's home, it was probably contained by a hearth. The hearth is the structure of bricks or stones surrounding the fire that keeps it (and the wood that fuels it) contained. A fire burns hotter when it is constrained within a structure of bricks or stone. There are even ways you can design a hearth to hold the heat of the fire—bricks and stones provide a thermal mass that absorbs the heat—and to throw that heat out into the room. The church can be a hearth that holds the fire of God's love, burning with you, among you, and between the other people in your life.

Can you imagine the church being a place that helps you burn hotter—as a community that absorbs that heat of the love of God together and reflects that heat out into the rest of the world?

The temptation in this historic moment of church reformation, widespread pastoral failures, denominational failures, faith deconstruction, and the realization that perhaps we have not created churches in which people are able to become "all flame" is either to jump from church to church looking for heat or try to burn as hot as we can all alone.

But starting a fire requires more than one piece of wood, and you have to start with small twigs and sticks and gently blow. And that is a lot of work for one person. If you are in a local church, you might consider grabbing a few friends and leaning into the practices within this book. This isn't the only way to start a fire, but if a few people within your community begin to live deeply into sharing vulnerably about the experience of the practices of constraint, you might end up sparking something.

The hope is then that your church could build a hearth to help you all burn even hotter. One of the most radical and helpful things you could do for your local church is to gather some others around you and pray together to become inflamed with the love of God. My deepest prayer in this season is that God will create little pockets of people who desire to become all flame.

If you are reading this and you have not yet returned to a local church in this post-pandemic age, there could be a temptation to just gather a few people in your living room, untethered from the church in any institutional or formal way.

You could begin there, I think. My caution is that in the long run this could feel like trying to build a fire in your living room without a hearth. I suppose it might work in the short run. But without a proper hearth, either the fire will be short lived or there is some chance that you might burn down your house.

The analogy might be breaking down a bit, but I want to say this: As broken and lost as the church in the West feels in this moment, we must learn to love her. Whatever we think about the institution of the church, if we are to have God as our Father, then, according to the tradition, we have the church as our mother.

There is a tradition within the church that has emerged throughout its history in moments of crisis. There are these moments in the history of the church when a small but prophetic charism emerges that invites people to burn a bit hotter, and it builds hearths for them to do so. We are in one of those moments. We are confronted with a growing awareness that the present typical forms of church simply cannot or will not allow us to become *all flame.*

But we do not need to leave the church to find the hearth. The traditions of monastic movements and religious orders, which are not outside but inside the church, have been building hearths for men and women since the fourth century. Religious orders, in all their forms—Jesuits, Dominicans, Cistercians, Franciscans, to name a few—share a particular spiritual framework for transformation and mission. They have found a way to help people burn hot.

Bring people together around the practice of constraints to nurture the experience of the love of God, and they will help one another catch fire. And the heat of these few who choose to live a deeper, more prophetic life end up warming the church.

Invite people to drink from the source of the river of the practices of the early church—a faith that embraced martyrdom—and they will have a chance to become all flame.

Create contexts to reflect the heat of God's love through these men and women into the world, and they will become what all of us were always meant to be—what Jesus said we would be—a light to the world (Mt 5:14).

It is to the practice of this tradition that we now turn.

CHAPTER TWO

FREEDOM

A MEDITATION ON THE JOURNEY TO OUR HEALING

I came into the world. Free by nature, in the image of God, I was
nevertheless the prisoner of my own violence and my own selfishness,
in the image of the world into which I was born . . . born to love
Him, living instead in fear and hopeless self-contradictory hungers.

THOMAS MERTON

Most people understand freedom as the ability to choose. Freedom, some say, is to be unhindered from outside influence. But we do not often speak about the *internal* influences, which we often cannot see but drive us in ways we wish they wouldn't. Most of us are good at hiding our inner desires and motivations—sometimes subconsciously even keeping them hidden from ourselves. But in order to be free—to be truly free to pursue what we really want—we have to be honest about what is really going on beneath the surface. This requires a great deal of humility. And this is why at the center of spiritual formation is the cultivation of humility.

The seventh chapter of Saint Benedict's Rule opens with the image of a ladder, a metaphor that describes the *degree* to which a brother in the community has moved toward humility and, because of that humility, toward greater freedom. In an informal lecture to novices at the Abbey of Gethsemani in 1963, Thomas Merton explained how archetypal the image of the ladder is: "In almost any form of spiritual literature you wind up being face to face with this ladder . . . you've got to climb this ladder. This is based on the fact, on one of the elementary truths of the spiritual life—you have to go from one place to another. We've got to go someplace."[1]

The most basic fact of the spiritual life is that you have to go from one place to another. Our journey, at its essence, is a journey toward humility because the only way out of the mess of competing desires and hungers and motivations is to go on a journey from self-sufficiency to knowing that we simply cannot gain freedom on our own. There is no good news without the part of the story where we talk about how glorious we were all meant to be—made in God's image, according to God's likeness—and how utterly unable we are to simply be what we actually are. We are unable to become in full what we have been promised that we *will* become. We must realize that we are helpless in this project of going from one place to another. God's rescue of us more or less hinges on the only thing that we could possibly contribute—the relinquishment of our *pride*.

And even when we can't let go of it, God will take it from us— we simply have to ask him to.

Pride, as seen in the Scriptures, describes the self-sufficiency that our first brother Adam and our first sister Eve picked up in the Garden, as the story tells us. Our recognition of how little we can do to mend the problem and our relinquishment of the idea that we could even begin to do so either in this life or in the life to come—well, this is the beginning of freedom.

The way up this ladder, as Benedict imagines it, is actually down.[2] And this downward journey is primarily one of allowing oneself to be healed by the fire of God's love.

Learning Humility

I've learned the most about humility and freedom from a recovering addict.

My friend Scott is six years clean. He now hosts meetings on Friday nights in a section of town about a mile from my own home where men and women walk the streets looking for a way to get their next fix. A few years ago Scott showed up at our little church, which was still very much in church-planting mode, and encountered the presence of God's love there. He was already sober, but he came at the invitation of a friend, and he received his inheritance as a son of God. Scott later told me that it was the first time he had been in a church in more than twenty years, and he was not expecting to find people there who loved him. When he shared about his journey of recovery and people leaned in further, he felt embraced by the family of God. We baptized him in the summer of 2020 in a horse trough in the park. Scott gathers addicts on Friday nights, reads a parable from the Gospels, serves pizza, and prays for people. It's glory.

Over the past couple years I have heard more of Scott's story. He talks about his years working in a suit and tie in Manhattan, living on the Upper West Side and building a company that sold for a lot of money. Eventually he was doing lines of cocaine on his desk at ten in the morning on a Wednesday. He threw parties that people talked about. And then, as these things go, this whole world he had created began to turn into something that he was not able to escape. He spent more money on drugs and parties than I have earned in a decade. His untethered "success" and wealth and his insatiable desire for fun created a prison whose walls had been built with the things that he *wanted*. It was a story of untethered freedom. And the things that he wanted enclosed him because he no longer just wanted them; he needed them.

And then his life fell apart.

The greatest gift of people like Scott in this world is that they mirror back to us with their lives some part of our own lives. I have never met someone, in all my years of pastoring and offering spiritual direction, who has not bumped up against a deeply held disordered desire that does not also eventually cause problems in their life. This is not how *all* our desires work. But we each have one or two desires that could lead toward destruction. In the spiritual formation tradition these are known as *disordered* or *inordinate* desires.

Most of us are able to hide the ways we have become prisoners of our disordered desires. And many of us are unaware that this is even happening. We are good at expressing those desires in socially acceptable ways. Or they operate on a level within us that creates just enough hum to notice, when we are paying attention, but not enough noise to be disruptive. But when the hum gets louder and calls for more attention—that's when the desire leads us down the broad road of destructive behavior. Perhaps you've noticed a humming on a deep level within yourself, which has made you wonder if there is something destructive happening.

These are *interior* disordered desires and they show up in different ways. Here are some examples you might relate to.

Perhaps you have felt unsettled by how much you have fixated on something. Maybe you did not get invited on the team or in the room or around the table, or your voice was not welcomed in the conversation—and it took weeks to get over it. Then you have this moment when you realize, "Wow, I really got stuck there!" And you wonder what that's all about.

Maybe that business investment you made with your savings account did not actually end up being a great decision. You are overwhelmed with shame at the financial loss, and you can't stop checking the balance of your retirement account.

Or you count calories and step on scales and exercise. Sometimes this is driven by a desire to be healthy. Other times, you have this image of your younger body in your mind that you are trying to get back to. It just shows up out of nowhere when you are looking at yourself in the mirror. Or rather, it's a conglomerate image of all the young bodies displayed in front of you, distorting your thinking about what a healthy body looks like. And you know this fact—you've read the articles on the dangers of Instagram—but you simply cannot let go of the possibility that you too could look like that. You stop eating ice cream. And you really like ice cream.

You show up at a friend's house, which is beautiful, and you drink expensive wine, and you have a really good time. You go to the bathroom and you are doing your business without any care in the world and then all of a sudden you notice how immaculately clean this bathroom is. Every corner is clean. There is a candle on the sink that smells amazing and the towels all match. *Where did they get those towels?* You don't think much more of it, but when you get home that very night and go into your bathroom to brush your teeth, you notice there are LEGOs in the sink, towels on the floor, and no one in this family can remember to put the lid on a tube of toothpaste. And so you begin tidying up, and then you find yourself soft scrubbing the bathtub. You have no idea why you are doing this at 11 p.m. until you step back and realize you wish your bathroom looked like your friend's bathroom. You turn out the light and go to bed thinking about how to remodel.

There are deep and often unnoticed desires that push us toward a way of being in the world. Most of these desires form in the early years as we learn to cope with how hard it is to be a human being. We're surrounded by other humans who themselves are trying to cope with how hard it is to be a human being. And when we take into account recent attachment science and how the things we fixate on are often the result of complex trauma, how we think about our *desires* takes on a new level of complexity. We need to have compassion for ourselves. We are full of so many desires, many of which are not necessarily *sinful* desires. But the way we act with those desires can cause destruction. And even when we do not realize how much force these desires exert, our life bends toward their satisfaction.

The bend is slight at first.

And then more pronounced.

And then it is permanent and we just learn to live with it.

Eventually, our desires become our masters. And we serve them.

This, by the way, is what the Enneagram gets at. Deep inside us we are driven by things we cannot name and memories that we cannot remember. They show up in the way we work and love and play. Or the way we do not work, or fail to love, or have forgotten how to play. The Enneagram tradition rests on an old concept that was emphasized in the early church long before anyone was talking about family of origin and first formation and what number you are.

These patterns of thinking and the subterranean forces they are attached to have never been far from the theological discussion about what exactly is the problem that we face. What was first articulated as eight evil thoughts[3] and later as seven deadly sins, now shows up, somewhat anesthetized, as nine personality types in the Enneagram. These all reflect the same ancient psychological insight: There are basic desires operating in us. We are not always in control of them, and they can push us toward destructive ways of being in the world.

The Passions

We use the word *passion* today in a way that would be unfamiliar to those men and women who went out into the desert to learn how to love and be loved by God. When we talk about passion we often mean "any very strong emotion, positive or negative. 'She has a passionate desire to serve the poor.' 'He was in a real passion when he killed the man.' 'She is a passionate lover.' 'He has a passion for chocolates.'"[4] But in the context of the journey toward freedom, the desert fathers used this term to describe something entirely different.

The early monastics tried to get at the heart of human emotions and existence. They were learning firsthand, in community, that there was something wrong with how they navigated their daily lives with one another. Modern psychology developed primarily unhitched from the spiritual, but it parallels the discoveries of men like Evagrius (a student of Origen, who was a teacher of everyone), Augustine, John Cassian, and others. They learned about "psychology" while trying to survive in the Egyptian desert off their shared earnings from basket weaving.

No wonder they learned how to pray.

The passions are desires and attitudes and sometimes-obsessive emotions that have carved out a special place in the room next to the deepest part of our self. And that little room is full of power. It is full of desire (*epithumia*) and resistance (*thumos*).

It is from this room where we learn to *want* things—both good and bad.

It's from this room where we learn to *resist* things—both good and bad.

This room is sealed up tight in a way that pressure builds like the steam in a steam-powered train. Desire and resistance. These forces power most of what we do with our bodies and our thoughts.

Imagine that the room has two valves where the pressure gets released. One of those is a slow-release valve that seeps out *desire* and *resistance* into our bodies, which in turn powers our most basic drives for security, intimacy, and control. This valve works like an IV drip: a slow, steady dose of desire and resistance every day. We hardly even notice.

The other is a quick-release valve—it's triggered by our trauma and our wounds in ways that we don't understand. It functions more like a waterfall that dumps a bucket of desire or resistance on top of us and then disappears as quickly as it came. It hijacks the chemistry in our brain, floods us with fight-or-flight responses, and causes us to do and say things we later regret. We wonder how we could be a person who just did these things. *Where did that even come from?*

With a little therapy, a healthy community, and people who love us, we can understand how this second valve works, and it can become less dangerous. But until we do that work it has its way with us and damages our relationships. It is why we throw things and punch walls or pillows or occasionally "lose our shit."

Sometimes we turn these valve handles ourselves. And sometimes it seems something else is turning the handles, and we feel completely unable to do anything about it. Like that little flare up inside of us when someone cuts us off on the road? That's in the vicinity of the passions. It's called *anger*.

If you've ever been so angry at someone that for a flash you imagined them dead or injured, or if you've ever thrown an object against the wall out of frustration in the middle of an argument with your spouse, or if you've felt so much anger that you've shouted into a pillow with hot tears or punched something or someone, you've experience what the Catholic catechism calls *wrath*.

That nearly obsessive checking of "likes" on the socials? The abbas called this *vainglory*. It is a form of pride where we seek the affirmation of others.

Pride itself is actually a little different. Pride is that feeling that rises up when you pat yourself on the back. The response that is most in keeping with our truest self—made to be *like* God—would be to pat ourselves on the back while also offering praise to God. This is almost never our first instinct. We have to *learn* to do this.

That incessant desire to upgrade? Early church father John Chrysostom would have called it *avarice*.[5] The pursuit of becoming an influencer? That's probably avarice as well—at least that's what Gregory the Great would tell us. Avarice isn't just a desire for wealth or possessions but for honors and high positions.[6]

I remember quite recently I had a little bit of joy rise up in me when I saw a public misstep of someone who had hurt me. It was completely unconscious, out of my control, and yet there it was, steam rising from that little valve in that little room. And once I noticed it, I had to name it. It came to my attention while I was practicing silence and solitude. It just darted into my mind during that time of prayer, which is how God speaks to me sometimes. I didn't feel shame or condemnation. I just realized that my thoughts about the situation were not in line with the love of God.

A similar struggle I face is feeling sadness when someone I admire does something great and gets public acclamation for it. This is a sickness of my soul. It's rooted in life experiences that I had no control over during my younger years. And yet, I've fanned a little flame of that sadness since as early as I can remember. It became an unconscious habit of my heart.

I share these struggles because they are true of my experience of myself—what good is there in hiding? These two things—joy over another's misfortune and sorrow over another's fortune—are known as *envy*. This is the emotion that gets triggered when you compare your dirty bathroom to another's candlelit porcelain paradise. (Is my own clean-bathroom fixation coming through? Surely you realize I'm talking about myself.)

And while pornography is now fairly ubiquitous in Western culture—one in three Americans seek out porn at least once a month—even just the thought of sexual fulfillment outside of marital union and intimacy would have been seen as rooted in *lust* among early theologians. They weren't afraid to name it as such. Most people who look at pornography are coping with trauma. It's a self-soothing technique of detaching from reality. It's terribly damaging, but it comes from a wound and often not from a conscious choice toward sexual fulfillment. It's just steam escaping from the room. And God wants to heal it. And God can heal it.

Wanting more of anything than we actually need (wealth, possessions, food, drink)—this is simply *gluttony*. I've never heard a sermon on gluttony, but the early church fathers talked about it—often through sermons about fasting—more than almost anything else in the spiritual life. If you want to pursue freedom as the desert fathers understood it, fasting is square one. We eat and drink a lot in Western culture. By any health standard we eat too much. Science is showing that we drink too much as well. This too is often a form of coping with unprocessed grief and loneliness. Being a human really is quite difficult.

I'm not a teetotaler, by the way. I love a good bourbon or a Manhattan cocktail. I drink Scotch with friends. And I also know there have been seasons of my life when the automatic two-finger pour of bourbon after dinner was me just coping with how hard life is. We used cloth diapers, for God's sake! *Where's the bourbon?!* Sometimes this level of coping is fine. And sometimes it isn't. Again, I feel no shame in saying this. It's just the truth about my life as it has unfolded during my adulthood. It's something I keep a close watch on. I fasted from alcohol for about eight months while writing this book and then celebrated with it during the last month of writing. Having deep spiritual friendships and processing these tensions with a spiritual director have been an important part of discerning when the coping is good and the gift of a good bourbon or Scotch is a gift from God, and when it isn't.

Lack of focus? Moving through the day randomly without a lot of purpose or structure or momentum? Sliding into an unnameable boredom with some degree of depression? Does this sound like an advertisement for some new raw/vegan multivitamin nootropic enhanced antioxidant smoothie subscription service promising to cure you one blended cup at a time? Evagrius of Pontus called this *acedia*.

These eight thoughts—gluttony, lust, avarice, sadness, anger, acedia, vainglory, and pride, as Evagrius named them—and their later rearrangement into the seven deadly sins do not necessarily define the passions, but they get us close to them.

These thoughts are the primary places where the passions are put on display. The passions fuel these thoughts but they lurk deeper than them—they seize "the thought and [whip] it into a frothy, obsessive commentary."[7] If the passions are the acorns that you step on and push under the soil, these eight thoughts are the oak trees those acorns become. The world is good at watering and fertilizing all those acorns (passions) until they become oaks (thoughts that lead us astray). Then the full-grown oak trees unfortunately drop new acorns. This is why it's hard to feel like we're making progress. These destructive thoughts, in cooperation with the passions that stir them up, reproduce themselves.

Who can free us from this?

Freedom is not merely learning how to cut down an oak tree—that is, learning to manage the thoughts and the sins those thoughts lead us to. Freedom comes from learning to recognize where the acorns are and having them rooted out by the love of God.

Thanks be to God.

The unhealed passions distort our ability to see the goodness of God in our own life, in the lives of others, and in the world around us. We are looking through a forest of oak trees trying to find one another. And we simply cannot see. And if we cannot see, we cannot love.

To say it more plainly: we are blinded by the passions. They block our field of vision. These passions and the thoughts that emerge from them run much of our lives. If our passions are managing our lives from that small little room adjacent to the center of our self, then we simply are not free.

The Great Physician

Most of our modern-day spiritual practices have forgotten that so much of the spiritual formation tradition rested on one essential truth: Christ alone is the physician of our soul. Often these lists of *vices* are used in the context of talking about sin. I'm not opposed to talk of sin. I don't want to go soft on it. But something has shifted in the way I think about sin over the past decade or so, particularly as I have done therapy, spiritual direction, and inner-healing prayer.

Most of our struggles with sin stem from unconscious, learned ways of coping with hard things in life. The earliest psychological tradition of the desert fathers helped name various forces at work within us, describing in detail the way these forces, these passions, exert their destruction on our lives. But what they couldn't see is the way these forces first develop as self-protective measures against a harsh world.

Of course, this is at least half the definition of idolatry, and our idolatries must be remedied. But we often forget that they have already been remedied. We forget that the gospel is a story about how those patterned ways of coping apart from God's loving presence no longer have power over us in the same way that they once did. These coping mechanisms, in the end, are actually more like wounds that need to be attended to. We can bring the wounds into the loving presence of God, who will heal us and exchange our distorted use of God's gifts for a well-ordered use of them. But this takes time.

Somewhere along the way we picked up the idea that our spiritual journey is about healing ourselves. Or, to return to oaks and acorns, we come to believe that maturing in the way of Jesus is about learning to chop down those oak trees. We imagine that on our journey "from one place to another" we move from a forest full of oaks to a cleared field of felled trees—and we go to church to learn how to swing an ax. Let's get to work! Or we take on spiritual practices to modify our behavior.

But this kind of life is too much of a hustle. The trees just keep growing.

The greatest temptation, and the greatest trick of the enemy, is to feel as though the goal of following Jesus is to rid ourselves of those wounds. It is the temptation to believe that we are meant to train until we feel strong enough to wield the ax and get swinging: "Let's cut down that envy over there!"

There is no doubt that we have a role to play in this journey of formation. We certainly have contributed to the growth of those oaks. At least I know I have. But, friends, we are yoked to Christ himself! And the burden is meant to be light. Our main work is *participation*.

God is the physician. When we are willing to disclose exactly where it hurts and trust God enough to open the wound in order to set the broken bone and stitch up the laceration, we're *participating* in that healing. As Dallas Willard points out, the yoke is meant to be light—but this implies that there is a field to plow. There is work to do. And there is soil to turn over.[8]

But what exactly is the healing work of Christ in our lives? How do we participate in that work? And how does this bring us into freedom?

In an interview he gave just before his baptism, my friend Scott put it this way,

> What has brought me to this point in my life, as a self-directed life, ended up not working out very well for me as I found myself deep in addiction. . . . You know, there is a beauty in that actually, because it is so easy for me now to access God's grace because when I was in total despair, and there was no hope, and there was no way out—I've now been able to come to a place where I live for his direction. My journey is that I started in recovery almost four years ago. And part of the twelve-step recovery program that I'm involved in . . . is a guide to how to live. It's a spiritual program and the foundation is: "I am unable to cope with addiction by myself." This was proven time and time again, that I just did not have the power to be able to do that. Over the course of my recovery journey, at first, I wasn't able to turn to God because what I thought of was the God of those earlier years of my life—I didn't know how to do it. I didn't understand it. But over the course of time, based on some difficulties that I went through, even in recovery, I was faced with the decision to turn to God or try to solve these issues on my own. When I started to pray I wasn't sure there was a God, but I was so desperate so I went ahead and prayed to him. Because of the pain I felt, I just kept doing it. And over time, it led me to the beginning of a relationship with God.[9]

One of the earliest titles of what is now referred to as the Big Book in Alcoholics Anonymous (AA) was *A Way Out*. The way out of addiction—the only way to become free—is to radically embrace one's helplessness. This is the first step of AA's twelve-step ladder. Scott stumbled on—tripped on it, really—Benedict's ladder of humility, inconspicuously embedded in AA's program. This was the only ladder that could get him out of the hole he was in. He discovered that freedom as we generally think about it is not actually freedom at all. We tend to think about freedom—in our late modern/postmodern/deconstructing world—as the absence of constraints. But the absence of constraints is exactly what landed Scott in the deep pit of addiction.

Scott's life can serve as a parable for our own lives. People who struggle with addiction to drugs or alcohol or sex find themselves coping with things that are not socially acceptable enough to continue in any respectable manner. But the rest of us are coping all the same, though perhaps at times to lesser degrees. And some of us are better at it than others.

Freedom Is Not the Absence of Constraint

Freedom is the ability to do what one *really wants to do*. Those whose unhealed passions are ruling them are no longer free. We're enslaved to nagging, recurring hang-ups, irritations, impulses, and attitudes: eating, drinking, working, sleeping, watching, hiding, demanding. And while many of us don't end up at rock bottom in despair, a large portion of our life gets swallowed up by the passions because they remain unhealed. We are mostly unaware of the extent to which we are ruled by them.

Every addict I've spent time with has told me that they would not trade their story for another. There is something that happens when you become aware that the passions are stealing your freedom, even when becoming aware comes at a great cost.

It turns out that when you lose your life, you end up finding it.

If my friend Scott's story seems too anecdotal, we can reach further back to the Cappadocian father Basil of Caesarea (from the East) and Augustine of Hippo (from the West). Basil was asking similar questions about freedom, and Augustine's life was much like Scott's. They all reached the same conclusion: those who allow the passions to rule their life are not free.

Basil of Caesarea was a fourth-century bishop in Cappadocia. He tells a story about a wealthy master and his slave. The master is completely entangled in the pleasures of a prostitute, but the slave does not pay any attention to the world of sexual pleasure. He is a slave, after all. He has had to learn within the constraints of his situation not to be wrapped up in the affairs of a lover. Basil tells us that this slave is "a slave in name only." The master, however, "has the name of master, but he has established his slavery by his deed."[10] Theologian Nonna Verna Harrison writes:

> So Basil asks, which one is more free? The master's mind is filled with obsessive thoughts and fantasies about the pros-titute. These thoughts, and the feelings that accompany them, drive his actions. He does not consider his wife and family, nor does he consider his reputation, which would have been very important to an aristocrat in the ancient world. He may be locked into the routine of a long-standing habit. So he is not free to use his reason to weigh the alter-natives and make a sensible choice. He is addicted, or, in Basil's language, enslaved.[11]

Saint Augustine lived the best life he could imagine in a bus-tling North African city. Parties. Lots of drinking. Lots of sex. Later, in his *Confessions,* Augustine observed that all that unte-thered freedom and the endless array of pleasurable choices created links in a chain that imprisoned him. What ultimately caused Augustine to fall apart, to hit rock bottom, was getting what he *wanted*. He had become enslaved to his passions, and what he first thought were choices resulted in a life that he was no longer actually choosing. He was trapped.

Augustine tells it like this:

> But I was bound not by anybody else's irons, but by my own iron will. The enemy possessed *my* wanting, and from it he had constructed a chain for me and constricted me in it. Inordinate desire arises from a twisting of the will; and in the course of slavery to this desire, habit forms; and through lack of resistance to this desire, a certain inevitability emerges. With these links, as it were, interconnected (and that's why I've called this a chain), a harsh slavery held me tightly in check.[12]

Here is the trajectory of how the passions keep us in bondage.[13]

First, our will—the part of us responsible for choosing—gets distorted. We become unable to discern when and how to release those valves in that little room next to the center of who we are. We simply do not know what the valves are for, so we turn them at random because we have to release them someplace. We begin to put them on automatic—desire and resistance get released destructively and turn into thoughts resulting in gluttony, lust, greed, envy, anger, and boredom, to name a few. We think, "I should have more money in the bank"—and this thought leads us toward overwork and overextension or even theft.

Second, we begin to serve these thoughts. We act with our body and make choices to satisfy them. We clean the bathroom at 11 p.m., unaware that we're operating in *envy*. We pour a couple of drinks after dinner, first because it's fun and we like the taste, and then because . . . well . . . it's just time for a drink. *It'll help me relax.*

Third, this way of life becomes a habit. We no longer know why we check our phone first thing in the morning—it's just what we do. There's a lot to say here about muscle memory and neuro-pathways, but that is somebody else's book to write.

Fourth, there is no real, sturdy resistance to this way of life. *Let's take out a second mortgage to remodel the bathroom.* Most of us don't live in community in a way that others can apply some resistance to the decisions we want to make, and so we just make decisions apart from the input of others.

Finally, the whole scenario becomes a necessity for us. It feels like the nagging sensation will not go away until we give into it—whatever *it* is. And we cannot break free.

And if we *must* do it, or we *cannot not* do it, then we do not have freedom.

On some level we all operate within this progression of unhealed passions functioning in compulsion and a lack of freedom with some part of our lives. The only way to heal from this progression is to find a place of connection in community where vulnerability has been normalized and all the problems we face with our unhealed passions are met with love, grace, and kindness.

Practicing Humility

The unhealed passions are healed through the love of God. We grow in our capacity to receive the love of God through growing in humility. Humility is a gift from God. But it can also be cultivated. The monastic tradition of living one's life in community with others with particular constraints is designed to cultivate humility. These men and women recognize that in order to be free they have to live in a way that regularly takes a look at the places in their lives where they are experiencing the least degree of freedom.

One temptation we face is to try to bring about our healing by shutting down our desires and passions altogether. They lead us to wayward places, after all. Let's put a lid on them! This line of thinking has made its way into much of the Christian subculture in the past half-century. My parents were not allowed to play cards or go to the movies. My wife went to a Christian high school where they were not allowed to dance. When we got married, the church she grew up in offered us the fellowship hall for our reception—but no dancing! Strict rules try to manage the real desires that live inside of us. But we can't simply pretend to detach from the parts of us that are full of desire by trying to manage our life with rules that prevent those desires from coming out.

The passions are there for a reason! In order to heal them, we need to get in touch with them. We need *desire*. We need *resistance*. And there is an important distinction between trying to eradicate our desires on the one hand and reordering and reshaping our desires on the other hand. There is way of practicing constraint that leads to the healing of our passions.

What *desire* is at the center of why I am living my life the way I am presently living it?

What *resistance* do I give (or not) to the things vying for my love that are not really worth receiving my love?

When we begin to answer these questions, we become aware of the oak trees in the forest and begin to see how they are obscuring our view of God and the goodness in others. What the desert fathers taught us, and the tradition they passed down through the monastic orders, is that we have to create a life that regularly invites God into the forest of those oak trees. We must live in a way that daily invites our loving Father to walk us through the forest and name the trees. We need to slow down enough to feel the acorns under our feet, get curious about what lies underneath, and invite the Spirit to dig in that particular place.

Those who practice a life of constraint in community seek to help one another pay attention to what is happening at the deepest level of desire, and they trust that this is the place where God is doing the healing work. We will talk about *how* the constraints get us to the work of healing in the next chapter. (Spoiler: It's about the love of God.)

All of this desire—heal it. Lord, have mercy on me.

My will *to make good choices?*—Thy will be done (Mt 6:10 KJV).

This life I am trying to carve out for myself?—Into Thy hands (Lk 23:46 KJV).

Who could ever free me of this? Thanks be to God (Rom 7:24-25). This is the journey of Benedict's ladder of humility.

Have mercy on me.

Thy will be done.

Into Thy hands.

Thanks be to God.

We will also talk further about *how* constraints help us climb or descend this ladder. But first, a word of caution. We cannot simply *practice* our way into healing. You can download that habit tracker app on your iPhone and check off all the things you want to do to be a better human. They can even be spiritual practices like sabbath and prayer and reading the Scriptures: drink more water, pray the Jesus prayer each morning for twenty minutes, do the midday exam prayer, wake up early, eat a healthy lunch, confess sins, practice sabbath, and so on.

But practices of constraint do not by themselves change us. The practices themselves do not have any formational capacity in the long term. These are simply external behavior modifications, which is fine for some things. I actually do need to drink more water. Practices are means (and sometimes techniques) that are meant to help us on our journey from the place we are to the place we are going. But changing our practices is not the same as spiritual formation. As Jim Wilder and Dallas Willard put it, "We have a terrible tendency to think that the means are the solution."[14]

The only solution to our bondage is the grace and the love of God and our *experience* of his grace and the love. We have to touch it. And our ability to touch the love and grace of God rests upon our experience of humility. Practicing constraints is the intentional cultivation of humility. In humility we can experience the love of God. In humility we keep ourselves in the love of God and wait for the mercy of the Lord Jesus Christ to bring us to eternal life (Jude 1:21).

CHAPTER THREE

CONSTRAINT

A MEDITATION ON THE EDUCATION OF
LOVE AND HUMILITY

We must ourselves learn to feel in each action
both our weakness and the help of God.

JOHN CASSIAN

The only way to freedom is through the experience of our be-
lovedness, our unique "being loved by" God. The only way we
can experience the love of God is in humility. And we have humility
when we have need, are willing to admit that we have need, and
receive the help and love of God. Sometimes the love of God comes
to us directly. But much of the time it comes to us through others.

Humility is necessary. But humility is something that we
have to learn. And we learn humility through the experience
of constraint.

There are two types of constraints—those we have chosen and
those we have not chosen. We *choose* some constraints in our lives

and we *consent* to other constraints that we have not chosen as practices of training our lives toward humility, so that we might be able to see the help of God in our weakness.

Any practices of constraint—spiritual disciplines, spiritual practices, spiritual workouts, living with others with a shared rule of life—must *solely* be in service of focusing our attention on the radical generosity and kindness of God in the midst of our greatest struggles. This is what eventually makes wholeness possible.

You and I breathe the breath of God. We are created to receive in ourselves the glory of God's presence. We are destined to love as God loves. These are the most basic facts about us.

But we have to *learn* to breathe with God's breath.

We have to *learn* to receive God's indwelling presence.

We have to *learn* to love.

Learning to Love

The primary way we learn to love is to watch the way that God loves us. We watch God love us in the midst of our unique circumstances and our particular form of the weakness that comes from being human. Again, God can love us directly, but he has also brought people around us to mediate his very own love to us. My own unhealed passions work against the love of God by isolating me from others, distracting me from attentiveness to God and others, and causing me to believe things that are not true about myself and others. The way that my passions are at work in keeping me from all that God is inviting me toward is probably very different from the way that they are at work in preventing you from responding to God's invitation. Constraints help us get a clear view of how our particular form of weakness is at work.

We can also learn to love and discover how God loves while watching God love others. This is one of the reasons we need community. But we cannot *know* the love of God until we have experienced it in our own unique particularity.

This is why our work as participants in our own formation is to grow in our attentiveness to God's ongoing cascade of love for us uniquely. We cannot watch God love us with attentiveness if our pride and ego create too much resistance to look at the act of God loving us. God is loving us *in* our weakness, and this is the place we often do not want to look.

To watch God love us, even when we are experiencing our unloveliness, requires *humility.*

If you find yourself in the weeds as you read this chapter—and there might be a few weeds ahead as we work through the philosophical and theological framework—those first paragraphs above are also meant to be the final word, at least in this book, about who you are and what God is up to in your life. They serve as a reminder of what we are doing in this work as we participate with God in getting to freedom through the practice of constraints. If I could set a notification within this chapter for you to go back and reread that opening section, I would. Come back to those opening lines as you need to. Bookmark this page!

We have a little more groundwork to lay before diving into our practices of constraint. We do this foundation-building work because it is easy to lose sight of *how* the spiritual disciplines (or rule of life) and constraints do what we want them to do for us. We all long for freedom in following Jesus. This is not the freedom simply to do anything we want but the freedom to choose what leads to what we ultimately want—to love and be loved.

We are often not aware that this kind of freedom comes through a process that feels like giving up some freedom. My friend Scott still goes to three or four AA meetings a week. This is part of the constraint on his life. But this commitment allows him to continue to choose what he really wants.

The Image of Love

As kingfishers catch fire, dragonflies draw flame;
As tumbled over rim in roundy wells
Stones ring; like each tucked string tells, each hung bell's
Bow swung finds tongue to fling out broad its name;
Each mortal thing does one thing and the same:
Deals out that being indoors each one dwells;
Selves—goes itself; myself it speaks and spells,
Crying Whát I dó is me: for that I came.
I say móre: the just man justices;
Keeps grace: thát keeps all his goings graces;
Acts in God's eye what in God's eye he is—
Chríst—for Christ plays in ten thousand places,
Lovely in limbs, and lovely in eyes not his
To the Father through the features of men's faces.[1]

This is Gerald Manley Hopkins's most famous poem. Literary critics and poetry professors regard it as one of his most important poems because it illustrates beautifully a concept that Hopkins leaned on heavily: everything in the world is unique.

There is nothing that has been repeated.

Every stone rings a unique ring when you drop it down a well. Every bell cries out its own unique name. And even if we share the same species designation with all other humans, there is an interior scaffolding that is unique to each person. Hopkins called this phenomenon *inscape*.

Theologically, this means that God loves you uniquely and that Christ is *in you* uniquely loving those around you through the particularity of your own life. You have a unique structure and inscape for loving because your life is shaped in a particular way through patterns and experiences that nobody else shares with you. No one else has seen all that you have seen. No one else has been wounded in the same ways that you have been wounded. Which means that no one has been in the process of healing in the particular way that you are being healed. No one else has been filled with joy in response to the exact moments that have filled you with joy. This is your inscape.

Of course, we share experiences with others. Part of the beauty of being a human being is that we are able to relate our experience to the experiences of another. This is how movements are born, by the way. Women in the church share the experience of trying to live and love in the context of patriarchy, but each woman has had her own experience, even when she doesn't yet know how to name it. We need spaces for those stories to be told. Black and brown-skinned brothers and sisters have a shared experience of feeling and being marginalized in a racialized world that favors whiteness. But anyone who has sat down and heard the stories of racism (both individual and systemic) knows that each individual's story is unique. Each person has a scaffolding of interiority that has been shaped by his or her experience. Each person has an inscape even in a room of people who have a shared story, history, or identity.

Hopkins was a student of medieval Franciscan philosopher Duns Scotus, from whom he got this idea of the uniqueness of each individual. Thomas Merton was also a fan of both Hopkins and Duns Scotus, and he drew on this concept of uniqueness in relation to what it means to operate in freedom. For Merton, you and I are only free to the degree that we are able to be exactly who we were meant to be when God freely loved us into existence. But becoming this person is not a passive affair: "God leaves us free to be whatever we like. We can be ourselves or not, as we please. We are at liberty to be real, or to be unreal. We may be true or false, the choice is ours."[2]

You are unique. God is uniquely loving you. You can participate in God's unique love for you. Or you cannot.

Stamped by the Love of God

On Christmas morning 2020 I eagerly anticipated opening a particular gift. I am notoriously difficult to buy gifts for. On more than one occasion leading up to that Christmas someone in my family said to me, "Dad—you are going to love the gift that Sadie is going to give you." Sadie is daughter number three of four. Even she said to me, "Dad, this might be the best Christmas present you have ever received." I was even more excited when, with a few curious questions, I was able to suss out that it was a handmade gift. My favorite.

I opened up Sadie's gift on Christmas morning. It was a print from a hand-carved wood-block style carving that Sadie had made in art class. It was an original carving of the likeness of Saint Ignatius of Loyola. (Is there anything better than when your kids *get* you?) The print itself was made by covering the carving with ink—which in this case was rubber, not wood—and pressing the ink-covered stamp onto a fresh piece of paper. The paper receives the ink, and that ink creates an image—an imprint of the original.

This is the metaphor that the early church father Irenaeus used to describe what it means that we are in the image of God.

Another example of this process is a wax seal on a letter, which bore the imprint of the king's signet ring. A king would write a letter and seal it with hot wax pressed with his ring. That letter could travel a far distance and arrive at its destination, where the recipient could check the wax seal to make sure the letter was authentic.

I have an old typewriter in my living room. I picked it up at a yard sale a decade or so ago when I was in a season of collecting vintage home goods. If you look closely at an old typewriter, each letter sits on the end of what is called a type-hammer. This is the part of the machinery that rises up and strikes the ink ribbon, which itself sits just millimeters from the paper. The hammer strikes through the ribbon and simultaneously imprints its likeness on the page while laying down ink within the bounds of that tiny indentation. Find a manual typewriter and watch this up close. It is a totally different experience than typing a text message with your thumbs.

When the early church fathers were working out what it meant to be a human being, created in the *image* of God, according to God's *likeness,* they recognized that we are a "type" of the One who has come before us. If there is an imprint on the page, there must be an original carved stamp. If there is an imprint in the wax, there must be a signet ring that made the imprint. Likewise, if we are an indentation of someone, then that someone is sitting on the edge of a type-hammer.

This is Christ. He is *the* image of God. We are made in the image of God. Christ himself is the model. We are the type. We are the still-wet ink on a page representing that original work of art.

Christ is the first human of all creation. All of us bear the same image—the image of Christ. We bear the image of God. We are, all of us, made in the likeness of Christ. This is universal.

And . . . we are each of us unique.

It is as if the color of each print is its own unique color, with ink or paint that will eventually dry in its own unique way, reflecting the light with particularity. God hands us a paintbrush while the paint is wet and gives us gifts (charisms) for cocreating the final image. "Every person is the painter of his own life, and choice is the craftsman of the work, and the virtues are the paints for producing the image."[3] We become participants in the work of displaying his gifts in us in the world on the foundation (himself) that he has provided. Our paint palette is full of his gifts and God himself is urging us with his own love to pick up a brush and paint.

But we can become immobilized by unhealed passions. We are in a room full of distractions and empty promises enticing us away from this work that we have been invited into. And throughout this room there are other less beautiful palettes. We are enticed by these other palettes and we begin to use their less beautiful and counterfeit colors rather than the ones that God has set before us. And when we try to paint with these other paints we end up covering over the image. This counterfeit paint was not made for this canvas. We paint over the original image with greed and envy, getting ahead in the world and caring only for our own needs. We layer in pride and vainglory, thinking that we ourselves can fix this painting. Eventually we turn away from the work of image-bearing altogether simply because it is so hard to see the original image after all those years of false starts and layers of paint that have begun to dry.

And Christ himself still sits in the chair as a model, never growing tired of waiting for us to gaze upon him once again, ever inviting us to the palette that he has provided, with colors so richly hued. He is ever inviting us to hold the brush and paint. He's whispering to us the truth of who we are. He is reminding us to simply look upon him and receive his love.

The Education of Love

What is the curriculum for learning the unique love of God for us? It is our very own life.

When I was twenty-eight years old, I wore a chef's coat for about a year. I was passionate about food and farming and our connection to the land. I still am. I wanted my life in the restaurant world to work, though I'm glad now that it didn't.

My life in a chef's coat fell apart because I was falling apart.

The restaurant industry is hard. There were some weeks where I worked seventy-plus hours. I tried to keep my work schedule to about sixty hours a week as at home I had two young children and a pregnant wife who would soon give birth to our third girl. I loved the work, but I only lasted a year.

There was one Saturday morning at the restaurant that I will never forget. The restaurant was full of people and there was a line out the door. People just kept ordering our Cloud-9 ricotta-filled pancakes. Each order was three pancakes and you had to cook them slowly on low heat—so they took a little bit of time on the griddle. The restaurant had experienced quick growth since it had opened just two years prior, and it was one of the only restaurants offering brunch. I remember looking at the griddle full of pancakes and seeing a dozen or so new pancake orders lined up. I was sleep-deprived, carrying too much stress, and I felt completely overwhelmed by the task at hand. My job as the one wearing a chef coat was to get the food from the kitchen to the people waiting for their food. But that day something happened to me that I had never experienced before. I handed off my responsibilities to a coworker for a few minutes, and I went out the back door into the parking garage and had a panic attack.

It was during this year that I first met with a spiritual director, Dave, who later also became a mentor to me as I learned the practice of spiritual direction. During one of our monthly appointments during the year I was working at the restaurant, Dave listened to me once again lament the pressures of my job, the long hours, and the panic I experienced from time to time. Then he leaned in to ask a question that radically shifted some things for me.

"Jared," he said, in a quiet yet firm voice, "I've been hearing you talk over the last few sessions about your desire to leave this job and find another. I wonder if you have considered the possibility that God might have something for you in the midst of it?"

This is something I had never considered. I had no framework for suffering, and I did not yet understand the love of God for me in the midst of that suffering. What I discovered in that year, probably for the first time in my life, or at least for the first time in a way that impacted me, was that I had real limits. And they were surfacing. I was fragile in places that I was unaware of. I could not conquer this, as I had done with so many other things.

What I now understand is that these moments—the ones when we bump up against the limits of our humanity—these are the moments (days, years, seasons) where God has the most access to us because pride simply is no longer possible. I was crying in the parking garage over someone else's pancakes! I felt a little humiliated by this. But reaching this moment of healthy humiliation—when I had no way out of the mess I was in—was the greatest mercy of God.

This is not the kind of humiliation that I felt in middle school when I got rejected for the basketball team or failed to do a pull-up in front of the gym class. Those were moments of shame. And shame and humiliation are not the same thing, at least not in the way the early church defined them.

I'm using the word *humility* to describe the experience of being brought low. It's that condition, as André Louf describes it, "in which one finds oneself flatly on the ground."[4] In the original sense of the word, *humiliation* is simply a state of abasement. Having a panic attack in the parking garage in the middle of the brunch rush was the experience of being brought low. I was completely unable to move forward.

What I began to learn (and am very much still learning) was that my weakness is not a deficiency in me; it is the condition in which I am meant to learn the love of God. It is in this condition that I learn the help of God. This is the part of our humanity that many of us have assumed is a glitch. But this is not a glitch. It's a feature.

This is what the desert fathers and mothers went out to the desert to discover. They went to the desert to learn the love of God, and they found it by discovering their limits and allowing the weakness in their life to become more visible to them. In learning the contours of their weakness, they were reminded of what we have always been meant to know: we are not meant to operate from a place of having everything. Because, if we have everything, we are in need of nothing. And if we are in need of nothing, then we cannot experience being loved. The experience of being loved requires that something fill in the gap. God created us with infinite need so that we might know that nothing small or temporary can fully fill us up. Only God can do that.

If we do not experience weakness we cannot experience the help of God.

We are meant to live in need of our Creator. This was how the relationship was set up from the very beginning: God freely giving of God's own self to the humans he had created. God giving so much to those first humans and yet establishing a boundary to their self-sufficiency. This one tree over here—don't eat from that tree.

"But I want to eat from that tree," they said.

"I have given you everything you need. I will provide for you." God replied. "This is how this relationship works. This is what keeps us connected. Let me be the one to fill in the gaps."

We often view the curse on the ground and the pain that was introduced to the process of childbirth in Genesis 3 as punishment. I do not believe that the hard labor for Adam and the painful pregnancy for Eve is punishment. It is pedagogy. It is education. God was teaching Adam and Eve about their human limits.

Their job was still to tend this garden—and now there were very real limits on their capacity to do it. They still were asked to be fruitful and multiply and bear the weight of reproduction. But here too they would experience the limits of their human bodies. If you've ever watched a woman give birth, or are a woman who has given birth, you know that in the few days following the birth, a woman wonders how she ever did it. I have heard some women wonder, in those first few weeks, whether they could ever do it again. It is a miracle—and incredibly sobering.

Both sweat of Adam's brow and the pain of Eve's childbearing are pedagogies in learning the lesson of weakness. It's an education in humility. These limits issued in the Garden are constraints through which God teaches Adam and Eve and you and me and everyone in between that we were meant to have need, so that God can fill it.

This is the story of the Scriptures. It's a love story. It's a story about reconnecting with the most basic fact about us: we are loved. And we were meant to live in the love of God. We were created to need God and to be joined with God in the place where God's love fills our need. Without the experience of this need it is doubtful that we will experience the love offered to us.

And when God shows up in flesh and blood, the kingdom of God breaks out by revealing what was always true: the love of God fills in the places left unfilled and unfulfilled.

The blind regain sight.

The deaf hear.

The lame walk.

The outcast is brought near.

The name for the state of awareness of the unfilled and unfulfilled places in our unique lives is *humility*.

Humility is simply awareness. It's noticing. It is being able to look at the infinite depth of the caverns inside of us placed there by God. There is something within us that is infinite because we bear the image and the likeness of God. We are meant to come to the place where we feel that infinite cavern and know that the only thing that could possibly fill it up is infinite.

Humility, as those early desert fathers and mothers described and lived it, is necessary in order to be open enough to meet God and then experience and be transformed by that love. The only thing, as far as I can tell, that God opposes, is the proud (Jas 4:6; 1 Pet 5:5).

Our journey toward this awareness will be both completely like everyone else's journey in that we will be confronted with our weakness and the grace of God, and absolutely unique because the shape of God's grace and love for you is specific to you.

And now we can finally talk about constraints.

What Happens in the Love of God?

When we have tasted the experience of being loved by God, the unhealed passions begin to heal and are redirected toward God. Remember that little room near the center of who we are full of desire and resistance? When we stand in the love of God, the built-up steam of the passions gets released in right, well-ordered ways back toward God and into the world in God-directed ways. And this redirected, outward release we call *love*. When we are in the love of God, we begin to love with the love being poured out into our hearts by God himself. We love with God-supplied love, which is really just the love of God flowing through us to others.

All the energy that once was wrapped up in bathroom comparisons and sad thoughts at other's victories in the world, or happy thoughts at other's mistakes, or obsessing over the crypto-currency market, or exploding in internal rage because our roommate ate the last few cookies, or being immobilized by our mistakes—all that energy now begins to be released and redirected through the act of loving.

The passions are not eradicated—they get healed, modified, and redirected.

The question on everyone's mind, of course, is how does this actually happen? How do the unhealed passions, which prevent the kind of love and loving that we so desire, become *healed?*

How do we, to return to the painting metaphor, gain the freedom to pick up the palette of paint that God has provided in a state where we can trust our desires because they are rightly ordered?

How does lust turn into worship?

How does envy get redirected toward celebration?

How do we become less greedy and able to love others in the way that God loves them, full of generosity?

How does anger become a courage so fierce and full of understanding that it melts resistance with compassion?

How do we spend less energy on obsessing over likes and follows and learn how to love and follow the leading of God in our everyday lives of dirty dishes and unmade beds and too-long commutes?

The primary focus of spiritual formation is learning the love of God for us. As we learn how to experience God's love, the passions naturally (and, because it happens by God's grace, *supernaturally*) get redirected. We eventually learn how to *desire* the things that lead to love. We slowly learn to *resist* the things that get in the way of love.

But this doesn't happen simply because we are trying harder or even because we order our day around a new set of practices. Habits by themselves will not spiritually form us. Formation toward being freed from the grip of the passions happens through the experience of being loved by God. God loves us completely and perfectly at every moment, which means we are never far from a masterclass lesson on love. It is unfolding right before us—*within us*, as Jesus might say. But we have to pay attention. We have to have eyes that can see it.

Constraint is the practice of learning to pay attention. This is you and me settling into that front-row seat—watching God love us—with pen and paper in hand ready to take notes. Or, maybe we just soak it in the first hundred times we watch it performed—that's fine too. We can save the notetaking for later once we know the storyline of God's love for us.

In this act of paying attention to the way that God loves us, we learn that God's love is uniquely shaped for us. We learn that Christ has stitched himself to our body, soul, mind, and strength. And because God has taken on the shape of *our* life through God's own humanity, we can take on the shape of God's life as we become like him. The work of Christ pouring himself out into the world—emptying God's self into creation through the incarnation—is God demonstrating what a human life looks like when living into the full capacity of love (Phil 2:1-13).

And he is still demonstrating it in his resurrection life, but now this is happening through us (Eph 2:10). You love with the love of Christ. I love with the love of Christ.

This kind of human life takes great joy in the joy of others, as seen at the wedding feast in Cana. It levels out the exertion of power in community, as Jesus preached in the Sermon on the Mount. It takes us out of our way for the inclusion of others who are marginalized, as Jesus demonstrated with the woman at the well. This kind of human life allows our love for justice to put ourselves in danger as Jesus did at the cleansing of the temple. It leads us to give up our will as Jesus did in the Garden of Gethsemane and to give up our life for the sake of friendship as he did on the cross.

But can we really live this way? Do we have the same capacity that Christ himself has? Not quite yet. But our entire life is growing toward this. And God is doing, and has already done, the heavy lifting. The restored infrastructure for this kind of love is already present within us. This is the gift of grace.

Training to See and Hear the Love of God

The practices of constraint (spiritual disciplines, rule of life) are meant to bring us into awareness of what is already true about us even before we know it: we need the experience of the love of God. We have always needed the love of God. We are healed by the love of God. We cannot love in a proper way without first being filled up by the love of God. To practice constraint for any other reason and without the awareness of this intention, I think, is entirely misguided.

To see the love of God we must first see our need for the love of God. And this is where the passions are actually helpful to us. Our passions, and the thoughts that emerge from them, are trying to fill our need for this love in ways that are within our immediate grasp but in the long run do not satisfy. We look for things to fill in the caverns that we know are there in our life: More food, more drink, a more beautiful bathroom. More sex. More likes. More money.

If you are not trying to meet your needs in some way, you have probably mistakenly been told that you ought not to desire such strong desires. Perhaps somebody called your desire a sin. But desire is not sin. Desire is a gift. And we can't shut down the bad desires without also shutting down some of the good ones. In shutting down desire we remove all the data points in our lives that indicate to us that we are trying to fill in an infinite cavern placed there by God himself. But when we pay attention to where our desires are leading us, we can see the ways that the passions are trying to direct our lives.

The goal of spiritual formation is not the eradication of our wayward desires. We are not trying to eradicate the passions. It is healthy to feel deep desire. The desire to be seen is good. The desire for intimacy—that's good too. The desire for our work to matter—it's good! So many of us grew up in Christian homes that didn't know how to talk about desire and instead tried to push it down and cover it up or ignore it altogether.

When the external practices of one's faith become more important than attending to the state of one's interior desire factory, eventually all that built-up passion steam finds the well-worn path of least resistance to the surface. For those of us who were trained to eradicate our desires, our first step toward healing the passions will be to first learn the power of desire by letting it run a bit wild, within some safe bounds of community, therapy, and prayer in ways that won't be harmful to ourselves or others. Many of us will need a season for allowing our desires to surface, and for letting those desires cause the passions to surface, simply so we know what we're dealing with. We need to feel our desires so they can become data points that help us understand how they are attempting to direct our life.

On the flip side, some of us know the power of our passions all too well. We have experienced being caught up and out of control in our desire and resistance. We have allowed the passions to rule our decisions and choices. We're adept at meeting our needs with what is within easy reach. We see a cavern of emptiness within us—and we know how to fill it. And this might actually work for us in the short term. The things we reach for actually do fill us up. But only temporarily. Just momentarily.

The spiritual formation tradition teaches us that over time, and with God's help, we can notice where these passions are directed toward temporary fulfillment and train them instead toward allowing the love of God to fill up what is lacking. Those same passions, once educated (modified) by the love of God, are redirected back to God in love. This is why those passions are a gift.

The formation and healing of our passions happens through the love of God. The practice of constraint helps us pay deeper attention to our experience of the love of God. This training in deeper noticing is what the early fathers and mothers called *asceticism.*

Asceticism

I have put off using the word *asceticism* until now because it's a word that has so many negative images waiting in the wings of our imagination. There were certainly ascetic excesses in the early years of the monastic tradition, and these excesses are often what come to mind when we hear stories of the desert fathers subsisting on bread and water and the food foraged around their cave.

Asceticism, from the Greek word *askeō* ("to train"), is the intentional training regimen for our body, mind, and soul toward the state of humility. Simply put, asceticism is the intentional practice of experiencing being at the end of our rope. This reminds us of our weakness and the grace of God.

Take, for example, the discipline of fasting. Dallas Willard is quick to point out that the discipline of fasting teaches us a lot about ourselves very quickly: "It will certainly prove humiliating to us, as it reveals to us how much our peace depends upon the pleasures of eating. It may also bring to mind how we are using food pleasure to assuage the discomforts caused in our bodies by faithless and unwise living and attitudes—lack of self-worth, meaningless work, purposeless existence, or lack of rest or exercise."[5]

Of course, we are supposed to depend on food. It's a gift from God. Our desire for food is not bad. But have you ever had a moment when your desire for food or alcohol was something that you felt in bondage to? I'm not talking about the occasional over-indulgence. We are meant to feast as well! It's good to overindulge from time to time. Jesus brought forth a bunch of wine when everyone was already a little inebriated. This is actually the proper use of food and wine—to experience it as a gift, to celebrate with it. But for many of us food or drink are not places of celebration but places of bondage that dull the desires rather than open them up to the gift that those desires are meant to be.

The constraint of food (or certain types of food) through fasting is an ascetic practice that helps such a person pay attention to what might be underneath the compulsion to eat or drink too much. The training (ascetic practice) gets us in touch with the deep weakness (pain, trauma, grief) underneath the act of grabbing what is within easy reach (sugar, booze, carbs, etc.) to soothe that weakness. The uncovering of what is underneath is the first step to healing whatever we are unable to see. The beauty of food and drink is that it does in fact soothe us. Praise God for this! This is what it is for—beyond basic sustenance. It should be celebrated.

But, when one removes the temporary fix of the soothing nature of food and the way we use it as unhealthy self-medication (as distraction from emotional pain), whatever unhealed passion we are trying to cover up will quite naturally make its way to the surface. Again, as Willard said, fasting "reveals to us how much our peace depends upon the pleasures of eating." It is as though the volume of desire gets turned up unless it is immediately satisfied. Remove the satisfaction, and desire becomes magnified.

This is how fasting works. And in general this is how *asceticism* and constraint work when applied to other areas of our lives. The unhealed passions surface more clearly when we are in training than when we are inattentive.

Most of us intuitively know that asceticism (what the Eastern tradition calls *askesis)* carries with it some practices of self-denial. And we live in a moment when self-denial in pursuit of deeper attentiveness to our life with God is not exactly a trending topic. Secular culture is currently providing a variety of models for self-denial and asceticism through exercise regimes like CrossFit and dieting. This is asceticism toward an entirely different end.

The practice of asceticism in the Christian tradition, which I am reimagining through constraint, leads us toward *learning* our way into humility. And in this learning, we can watch more closely the way God loves us in our places of greatest weakness. It is the love of God that fuels the re-education and healing of the passions and ultimately wins for us our freedom.

Let's review where we have been.

- We are destined to become humans who love as God loves. In following Christ we are learning how to do this. We are participants. God invites us to pick up a brush and paint.

- We learn love primarily through watching the way that God loves us and secondarily through watching the way God loves others. God's love for us is both universal and unique to each person.

- But we have these passions (desires and resistance) that in their unhealed state lead us away from the practice of paying attention to God's steadfast love—a love designed to be on display for us, especially in our weakest places. As we satisfy these unhealed desires with temporary things and feed our resistance to the work of learning, we end up trapped in a life of inattentiveness to the love of God. We simply stop paying attention to the way that God loves us as our attention becomes wrapped up in other things. This is often due to the shame we feel because we know deep down that we are in the grip of the unhealed passions. We paint with other palettes and inferior paint brushes. This is the foundation of what the Scriptures call idolatry.

- We end up trapped because when we blindly follow our unhealed passions they get embedded into our habits. They become normalized into our everyday behaviors. We reach for the same paint brushes over and over.

- We become slaves to these habits and begin to live them in a way that becomes automatic. We do things without thinking. Some will eventually become things we can't *not* do. And this is not freedom.

- The only way out of this is to witness God loving us in the midst of being trapped. Christ is in the room lovingly gazing at us even while we sling inferior paint!

- But, in order to watch the way that God loves us, we need humility. In our pride and self-sufficiency we will not be able to see God loving us in our weakness. When we are full of pride, we cannot bear to look on our own weakness. But this is the very place that God is standing. We keep turning away from the image-of-God canvas on which we are meant to paint. In pride, we will often attempt spiritual practices as a tool to better ourselves but not as a means to learn humility. We strain out gnats and tithe our mint. And this too will fail. It's just another set of paints that looks like the real thing but isn't.

• • •

If we begin practices of constraint knowing that the purpose is to reveal our weakness rather than to conquer some bad habit, then we're practicing asceticism in the tradition of the desert fathers and mothers. Without the intention of learning humility, we might form better habits, but this is not the same thing as spiritual formation.

When we choose constraint or consent to the constraints already present, we have to reckon with the fact that we are not getting what we want. But once we realize that we are not getting what we want, we are much more in touch with our desires because they are now right in front of us rather than being masked by any number of strategies that we deploy. When this process is paired with prayer (solitude and silence), spiritual companionship in friendship or spiritual direction, and a loving community, we are able to do the work of deeper noticing. We can invite God to speak to us and allow God's love to begin to heal the unhealed passions:

What is this raging desire?

And why is it there?

What purpose does it serve?

And how might God want to direct that desire in the service of love?

The spiritual formation tradition and the practice of *askesis*—the practices of constraint—teach us that in order to be free, we must first come to a place where we are able to *see* the weakness of our inner lives and receive the grace of God there.

We practice silence and we're immediately confronted with a low rumble of uneasiness and anxiety. We spend some time in solitude, disconnected from the energy and presence of others, and we discover perhaps a need for attention that we otherwise would not be able to see. We stop drinking wine for a month and we become aware of a low-hum angst we feel that we've learned to cover up with that second or third glass. We enter into these seasons of training to uncover what we presently cannot see and to allow whatever weakness we're afraid of to simply come to our attention. And then we can begin to pray and talk with our fellow travelers and get curious about what, if anything, God might want to begin to heal.

The practice of constraint allows us to be confronted with what is actually true about the unhealed desires, particularly the ones that feel out of our control. We have to stand in front of the painting and look at all the ways we've painted over, with inferior paint, the image we've been given. And when we can accept that this is so and turn toward God, we are standing in a place called *humility*.

In this place we now have the eyes to see and the ears to hear the unique way that God loves us. And then, when we are no longer gripping the counterfeit palettes of paint, we can simply watch God love us.

CHAPTER FOUR

PRACTICING CONSTRAINT

CHOOSING AND CONSENTING

Any theory divorced from living examples . . .
is like an unbreathing statue.

GREGORY OF NYSSA

It is now time to move toward the practice of constraint. Read the second half of this book with others who already love you and care about you or with a few people that you don't mind growing in love for. Either one will work. But what will not work is for you to proceed alone.

The constraints in this book are drawn from the stream of monastic spirituality and have been practiced by a variety of religious orders throughout history. The spiritual disciplines found in the classic works on the topic all pull, roughly, from the same tradition of asceticism. There are simply some *essentials* of the spiritual disciplines and the practices of constraint that have been handed down to us. Each generation adds or subtracts or preserves from the tradition and contextualizes these practices for the cultural moment.

In short, I'm recontextualizing, but there is nothing new here. We are standing within the *tradition* of the practice of constraint. It's important to know that others before us have been down this path. Tears and heartbreak may visit you in the weeks and months to come as you and those around you seek out this way of life.

The way of life of constraint is filled with joy. But first we have to die.

Each chapter in this section closes with a few practical steps to take, whether you are practicing these in a local church or a living room community group, or sowing seeds of these practices into the life of your home as a parent. If you are in this last group and are wondering how to plant these seeds in your family, some particular care is required.

As a parent, I've been trying to plant little seeds of some of this work in the life of my own family. How do we even begin to talk with our kids about constraint without capitulating to that easy temptation toward rigidity and legalism? This is a very delicate process that will probably take years of mistakes and adjustments. At least it has for us.

The primary tool for parents' attentiveness to the spiritual formation of their children is a parent's own life of transformation.[1]

And conversation. Endless conversation. Which means you need time. Leisure time.

We've talked in our family about silence and solitude and created rhythms in our home to try to make this practice possible. These rhythms have changed throughout the years as our kids change. We've taught our kids to pay attention to what is happening on the inside, and they know that in their inner life is an ongoing invitation to the love of God. We've leaned into simplicity in ways that have been great. And, now that I have a college-aged daughter who has been able to give me some good feedback (which I asked for), I wish I could go back and do some things differently. This is just what parenting is.

There isn't any parent who is trying to create an environment of spiritual formation who will not also, at some time, realize that adjustments need to be made to the way it is being rolled out in everyday life. In the life of a family the work of spiritual formation almost never looks very formal. There is something still very compelling about Deuteronomy's instruction to teach our children diligently—we do it while sitting in our home and walking along the road, in the early morning hours and in the closing moments of our day (Deut 6:7).

We've talked in our home about the inner work of formational healing (see chap. 10). This has paid off with what I would call an emotionally robust environment (insert grimacing emoji)! It's not always easy, but we are very much committed to God's healing work in us. We've shared pretty openly with our kids (with appropriate vulnerability) about our own process of "doing the work" in counseling and therapy.

Our regular practice of faults and affirmations (see chap. 9) has shaped our family life. We've laughed and cried over dinnertime confessions and affirmations.

We've talked about sexual desire, marriage, and the real option of lifelong celibacy with our teenage girls in, I hope, a winsome way (see chap. 7), while also framing those desires within the context of our life of following Jesus. Our kids have watched us learn how to love one another as we've navigated challenges in our marriage. We have been (age-appropriately) open about these challenges. Our kids know that marriage is about formation and learning how to love.

And we have certainly made mistakes in our home. As you gently guide your family toward a countercultural way of life (celibacy anyone?), you will also, I suspect, make some mistakes. There will be mistakes in your words, your reactions, your timing. Parenting is one of the most humbling experiences of my life.

But God's help will meet you in your weakness.

If you are a local church leader or pastor, there are some specific invitations for you also as you lead those entrusted to you toward the practice of constraints. Lean into this work slowly, with a few close friends or leaders within your church or colleagues before trying to rally your church behind this deep, interior work. Live into some of this for a season with a handful of people around you. There are resources available at www.orderofthecommonlife.org to help you.

Start a small fire with just a few. And then slowly expand the invitation to other leaders and eventually it will slowly work its way through the life of your church. This is meant to be slow work. So build slowly.

If you are hosting a small group in your living room, create space to let people linger with each practice. There are six practices of constraint that I've been field-testing in groups for the last five or six years. But this is not a six-week study. You could spend a month or more on each of the practices. Things will come up, so move slowly.

There are questions to help guide a group discussion at the end of each chapter. I also invite you to consider joining one of our free community leader apprenticeships offered on our website. My desire is that this conversation bolsters the work of the local church. I'm writing this in a moment when many people are finding it challenging to reengage in the local church given the overall reckoning within American evangelicalism. If you are not engaged in a local church, I'd still love to give you resources for gathering people around these shared commitments of constraint.

The Immediate Objective and the Final End

There is a difference between putting your hand to a task with intention and expecting an immediate outcome and putting your hand to a task that is in service of something else. The goal of mixing flour and water and yeast into a bowl is not simply to bring those three ingredients together. We're baking bread here! The mixing is an immediate objective, but baking bread is the final end.

There is the immediate task of turning up the soil and adding some compost before you plant your seeds, but the final end goal is harvesting.

The same is true of the practice of constraint. There are immediate tasks—these practices—to attend to, but these are only the means to an end. The goal of constraint is our freedom.

It is the freedom to love, unhindered from the unhealed passions, mediated by humility, empowered by the love of God alone.

Within the monastic stream this is known as *purity of heart*. Purity of heart is being freed of the unhealed passions. John Cassian wrote, "As I have said, in every art and discipline a particular target is paramount: that is, an end point for the soul, a constant intention for the mind, for no one will be able to reach the objective of a desired goal unless he keeps this target in focus with complete attentiveness and perseverance. . . . Indeed our aim, that is, the target, is purity of heart, without which it is impossible for anyone to reach the ultimate goal."[2]

Cassian's ultimate aim was *union* with God. It was a journey to becoming "partakers of the divine nature" (2 Pet 1:4). Cassian bridged the gap between the monastic tradition in Egypt and the Christian East and the first developments of the tradition in Europe in the early fifth century. Cassian's work later informed the work of Benedict—and everyone after Benedict drew from Benedict.

The final end (or destination) might be *union* with God, but no one can set out on a life of discipleship with simply the goal of union with God. It's far too general. It's hard to persevere in the pursuit of union with God. But persevering in confession and the affirmation of others? That's a little more bite sized. I can do that with a few people around a table. Confession, for example, is an immediate means to a more distant goal that is harder to stay present to.

The practices of constraint are simply the activities we engage in (mixing flour and water and yeast, tilling up the soil and planting seeds), but they are *for* something else (making bread, harvesting what we've planted). And there are further ends that we might also imagine. The bread might be our contribution to a shared meal, for example. If you find yourself focusing too much on the activities of constraint, just keep in mind the final end of loving and experiencing the love of God.

In both choosing and consenting to the practice of constraint, remember that these are not practices we're trying to perfect or even get better at. We're participating in creating conditions that support the work of receiving purity of heart, which comes as a gift from God and as a fruit of being in community with people who are oriented toward the same ends, with common objects of love.[3] At the risk of saying the same thing over and over—this is one more reason that practices of constraint, or any practices that lean toward asceticism, must be done in community (river, womb, hearth).

Purity of heart is birthed in love. And you cannot love alone.

A Word of Caution

Spiritual practices and asceticism can easily become indulgent. Sometimes we gain a greater uplift in our spiritual life knowing that we have accomplished a spiritual practice than we do in resting in the work of God in Christ in us. This is a subtle but dangerous trap. Our up-and-to-the-right flavor of Western Christianity is particularly susceptible to it. Some of the current cultural understanding of how rule of life and the spiritual practices do the work of formation often leans more toward self-actualization than self-emptying.

As I hope to make clear in the rest of this book, if our performance of the practice of constraint is making us feel stronger, or if we begin to compare ourselves to others, or if we feel a bit of self-satisfaction because of our "spiritual progress," then we might be using the practices toward an altogether different goal.

This counterfeit goal should be abandoned.

Thomas Merton tells about his first few years at the Abbey of Gethsemani. He recounts how much satisfaction he felt during those first few years in being quite astute, not in prayer or the choir but in spreading manure in the garden. We'll find self-satisfaction in anything! For a Cistercian monk, manual labor is part of the spiritual practice. It's a *means* of learning humility. When the manure spreading became a source of accomplishment,

Merton later reflected, it fed his pride and needed to be approached with a different attitude.

It's a funny story thinking about Merton, one of the most prolific and important religious writers in the twentieth century, taking pride in his ability to spread manure. But I think we get it. We too can easily slip into the equivalent of measuring out mint, and cumin, and dill—something Jesus railed against—in our practice of solitude, sabbath, confession of faults, or discernment.

The shortest way to be on watch for this is to ask a simple question: *Am I feeling satisfied by something I am doing or by something God is doing in me?*

Consenting

For this reason I have framed half of the practices of constraint as ones that we ourselves do not initiate. Rather, they are constraints that are already present in our lives. Our practice for these particular constraints is one of *consenting* to the constraint in a way that allows for the formational capacity of those constraints to emerge. We are formed by the constraints that come to us.

I've been heavily influenced in this idea of consent by Father Jacque Philippe, who is part of a modern-day Catholic community, the Community of the Beatitudes, founded in 1973. He writes about consent as an interior attitude, a disposition of the heart in the face of things we find unpleasant about our circumstances and situation. We can even consent, says Fr. Philippe, to things we do not like about ourselves. Consent is an attitude of humility. It recognizes that we cannot control our lives, but we can allow the things that are happening to shape and form us. We can consent to hard marriages, tough financial challenges, even illness. All of these provide limits to our lives that end up becoming for us what ascetic practices can become—a crucible for teaching us how to surrender. And surrender grows our capacity to love.

We are often not aware of the constraints already built into our lives. I'm simply trying to help us see them for what they are—or what they could become—such that they can do the formative work they are meant to do. Once the everyday constraints of our lives emerge from hiding—that is, once we stop pretending that they are not there—we can embrace them.

We so often attempt to push beyond the limits and built-in constraints of our lives. Mothers and fathers of young children learn this quickly as they adjust to the constraints that a new baby brings into the home. As those children grow, we become present to constraints passed down to us by our family of origin—the unspoken trauma that has peppered our own stories. As we grow older still, we bump up against the natural constraints of our bodies. I now run a 10K a full six or eight minutes slower than I did a decade ago. I could push through it and try to catch up to my younger self, but then I'd injure myself.

Our life is full of constraint.

Participating in God's slow work in us happens primarily in the concrete situations in which we find ourselves. Take a moment to think about the most challenging things you are facing right now. I am nearly certain that at the center of the challenge is a constraint.

What constraints are present in your life that are completely outside of your control?

● ● ●

In these concrete realities of our life, as it truly is, we find our weakness—and the help of God. We never live a single day without the possibility of discovering our dependence on the help of God.

So, if constraint and weakness are so prevalent and always available to us, why should we pursue more of it? Why can't we simply deal with the constraints already in front of us? Why do we choose further constraint?

Here's an image to clarify the difference between *consenting* and *choosing*. Imagine sitting underneath a shelter as the skies open up with a downpour of rain. The clouds dump water without much warning. Now imagine intentionally stepping out from underneath your shelter because you want to dance in the rain. You are *choosing* to let the downpour overtake you. You could remain dry, but you choose otherwise.

Now imagine that same storm at an outdoor wedding. The bride and groom are walking down the aisle, the air is thick with humidity, and everyone is praying for a quick end to the service because the rain is just moments away. Just an hour ago your favorite uncle said to you as you took your seat, "It's going to rain very soon . . . I can feel it in my elbow." And just as the new couple is announced, the heavens open up and the rain pours. Most people make their way to the nearby shelter—but not the bride and groom. They embrace it! They do not let the rain spoil the moment. They *consent* to what is already happening, and like improv artists they work it into their wedding memory. They begin to dance.

Choosing to step out into the rain and consenting to being caught in the rain both result in getting wet. But how each of these situations unfolds is worthy of our attention. I hope you will see that we need both of these scenarios to do their work on us. Most of us are in a storm of constraints right now and the practice of choosing constraints will help us grow in the practice of consenting to the constraints that are already in our lives.

Let's go find some rain. *Come, Holy Spirit.*

Part Two

CONSTRAINTS
WE CHOOSE

CHAPTER FIVE

SILENCE and SOLITUDE

CHOOSING THE CONSTRAINT OF
THE PRESENT MOMENT

The Freedom to Rest

Whoever hammers a lump of iron first decides what he is going to make

of it, a scythe, a sword, or an axe. Even so we ought to make up our

minds what kind of virtue we want to forge or we labour in vain.

ABBA ANTHONY

In the neighborhood of our first home in central Ohio there is a small ravine that, if you aren't a local—or a warbler, you'd never know was there. It's called the Walhalla Ravine and it lies between two north/south roads. At the bottom of the ravine is Walhalla Creek and Walhalla Road.

It's a sanctuary.

Years ago I was walking the ravine as I did nearly every week for prayer. I loved the canopy of trees above me and the quiet the ravine provided as I tried to work out my vocation as a pastor while also working at a job I hated on the campus of Ohio State University. Ohio State is a wonderful institution. I just didn't like sitting behind a desk. I was beginning to lean into pastoral ministry bivocationally. That is where I was coming alive. It was becoming clear that pastoral work and the care of souls was my calling. I just couldn't make sense of how it was unfolding.

These were formative years in my adult life and much of that formation was worked out in the Walhalla Ravine on walks with my pastor or my spiritual director, but mostly with myself. I'd slip into Walhalla and hide for thirty minutes before transitioning from the work I loved and was growing toward to the work that paid the bills and provided a holding pattern in a season when I needed it.

My entry into the practice of solitude and silence didn't happen on a retreat at a monastery. I came to solitude and silence in desperation in the everyday "liturgy of the ordinary," as Tish Harrison Warren has so beautifully articulated it.[1] I came to silence and solitude with three little girls playing dress up all hours of the day. I sought out silence and solitude in the early morning hours after spending the evening with my kids sitting on my lap while I read scores of picture books to them at bedtime and then cleaned the kitchen. I found solitude as a place of refuge when my wife, Jaime, and I could not find the right words to say to one another that would heal the wounds we had inflicted. Marriage felt hard for nearly a decade. I didn't know how to fix it. I was just beginning to scratch the surface of the healing that God was doing in me.

And my basement kept flooding when it rained. And we were always running low on money.

Solitude and silence didn't come for me from the comforts of quiet, peaceful, middle-class privilege, as it is often Instagrammed. For me it was desperation. I came looking for God to *do something* in that space. And he eventually did. I just never understood what was happening or why I was drawn into this silence where I would turn my heart to God and find, eventually, that he, too, had turned his heart toward me.

I had run out of words for prayer. I had nothing to say. Most of my prayers in that season were tears.

One day while walking through the Walhalla Ravine I saw an older man sitting on a park bench near the creek. He was looking up at the trees through binoculars and it never occurred to me that he wasn't actually looking at trees. And so I asked him, "What kind of tree are you looking at?" He smiled at me and said, "I'm not looking at the trees. I'm looking for birds!"

"Oh," I said. "And what kind of birds are you looking for? Have you seen any birds today?"

"No, not today. But I'm looking for warblers. It's the season of the warbler migration. But no, I haven't seen anything today."

"How long have you been out here?" I asked.

"I've been out here a few hours already. But no warblers today."

I'm a pretty good conversationalist. But like in my prayer life, I was out of words for this birdwatcher and so I just stood there awkwardly.

And then he broke the silence. "You know, the warblers come here every year. There are forty-one species of warblers in North America. And almost every single species stops right here in the Walhalla Ravine every spring."

This guy, and this moment, felt like they were right out of a movie. I wasn't very interested in what he was saying. "Wow," I said. "That's interesting." And then I began to walk away.

"You know . . . I've been coming here to watch warblers for twenty years. I haven't seen anything today, but over the years I've seen twenty-eight different species of warbler right here from this bench." He chuckled a little. "The funny thing is that if I never came and sat on this bench with these binoculars, I'd never see a thing. The key to looking for warblers is that you just have to keep coming back to watch for them. You just have to keep coming."

And as I walked away I heard God say to me, "This is what I'm doing with you. Just keep showing up."

I think that old man was as close to an angel as anyone I've ever met.

The Constraint of the Present Moment

If you were a blacksmith and had a lump of raw steel, you'd want to know what you were going to make with the steel before putting it into the fire, as Abba Anthony said.[2] What are we trying to form within the practice of solitude and silence?

Awareness. Attention. Love. *Rest.*

These are all words for the basic idea of *presence.* What we really want in the practice of solitude and silence is the presence of God. Silence and solitude is simply the practice of being alone with God and not needing to say anything. We come wanting to be filled up and nurtured. We want an experience of God. We want to pray. We want to speak with God and have God speak back to us. But what we often get when we finally carve out the space to be alone and have a little quiet is noise. It's that inner noise of unmet expectations and failed dreams and little whispers that remind us how disappointing we are to others, or how disappointed we are in ourselves. The moments of silence are often filled with nagging questions and the natural overflow of an active mind.

Try a little quiet right now and see what happens. Take five minutes and sit quietly, then go to the next page.

Am I doing this right?

What about dinner tonight?

That deadline is approaching. I feel so behind.

Maybe I should read a different book.

I'm hungry.

I feel like falling asleep.

We come into silence wanting to "see a warbler" and what we experience is often just wind blowing debris into our line of sight. Our most consistent experience in silence and solitude, at least in the beginning, is distraction. But when we come back to the practice of noticing what is happening in the midst of that distraction, and when we stay attentive to the storm that distraction can bring to the silence, we begin to engage in what the formation tradition calls "contemplative prayer." It's a kind of prayer that actively opens up to the process of being attentive to what is happening in the present moment. In all the chaos of the present moment, which we easily become aware of in a moment of silence, contemplative prayer is becoming present to the moment that we are in and holding that moment prayerfully before God.

The distraction is normal. And it is also an opportunity.

The distraction within the practice of solitude and silence is something we often very quickly run away from. Becoming present to all those thoughts, which we have been ignoring with our busy lives and our habit of picking up our phones 340 times a day, can be terrifying. But in the practice of solitude and silence we train to stay in the moment.

What will we find there, when we really pause to listen, when we come into God's presence without a list of things to talk about? Is there pain? Is there boredom? Will God do something? And what if he doesn't?

The immediate objective of solitude and silence is to stay in the present moment and notice what comes up. This process of noticing is our first set of training wheels in learning humility. But staying in the moment turns out to be quite difficult. It seems counterintuitive, but the contemplative tradition and the practice of solitude and silence as asceticism say that the way we become free of all these obsessive thoughts that we meet when trying to find God is to practice sifting and sorting those thoughts. We learn humility by engaging in this work because this work is really slow work. But our desire for God becomes strong enough to help us stick with it.

Our first practice of constraint is that of constraining our attention to the present moment while beginning to learn to allow God to give us the grace to notice what is happening in us and to us in *this* very moment. We cry out to God *for* the present moment. We say to God, "I need your help sorting and sifting through all the thoughts and agitation and distraction that pour into my heart and mind when I attempt to come into your presence and simply be with you."

Eventually, God begins to show us that this cascade of thoughts— remember, *thoughts* are what spring from the *passions*—is nearly always operating in the background, even when we are not aware of them. Oaks come from acorns. The little steam room is always pumping out desire and resistance. As we learn to sift and sort those thoughts in God's presence in the place of silence and solitude, we begin to notice how those same thoughts are driving our attention and actions in the middle of our workday, at the dinner table, and in the night hours when we cannot sleep. They show up just below the surface when we're late for that appointment or glance at our bank account or watch another person get promoted ahead of us. It's all very subtle. But these thoughts take up more space than we realize.

Silence and solitude and the constraint of the present moment train our attention and our awareness of all the competing and compelling voices working to direct our next move.

I do not believe there is any freedom without engaging in this battle.

This is why Jesus was himself compelled into the solitude and silence of the desert by the Spirit.

Learning to Sift and Sort

In nearly every tradition that has taken the need for constraint to heart, you will find the practice of silence and solitude at the center. You will also find discussion of what to do with distraction.

Rest assured. You are in good company if you find the practice of solitude and silence difficult.

In the earliest tradition of the monastic stream, in the final decade of the fourth century, a monk named Loukios wrote a letter to one of the leading spiritual guides in the Egyptian desert. The recipient of this letter was Evagrius of Pontus, who had become well-known for his wisdom about what to do with distraction—particularly the kind that took on an edge of accusation, obsessive thoughts, or enticement toward sin. Younger and less experienced monks would come together around Evagrius to listen to him teach about what it looked like to struggle with these thoughts over the long haul. Again, we see that from early on the men and women who went out into the desert to pursue solitude and silence came together to talk about it and share stories of their experience. As tempting as it might be to practice solitude alone, there are almost no positive examples of where this has been fruitful—other than some fanciful stories. Even Saint Anthony had visitors throughout his twenty-year stint in the wilderness.

Evagrius lived through an emotional and physical breakdown during his years in Jerusalem when he was a student of the Cappadocian father Gregory of Nazianzus.[3] He was counseled toward monastic life in Egypt by an older woman, and he began his journey of healing through the practice of solitude and silence and spiritual friendship with others pursuing the same way of life.

Evagrius used a framework of *talking back* to the voices and thoughts that entered his mind along the lines of the passions. Evagrius and his contemporaries lived in a time when those inner voices were thought to be demons. There is much theological and psychological research working to get at the heart of what is happening with these distracting thoughts, particularly the ones that feel so accusatory. There has also been substantial movement away from talk of demons in favor of more psychological explanations—memories and trauma—that tend to surface once we have removed the distractions around us.

It shouldn't surprise us that the men and women who practiced ascetic constraints in those early years developed a fairly robust understanding of the "demons." Much of the monastic world at that time began to focus on what to do with the thoughts that emerged while trying to pray.

Part of the reason our conversation around these accusatory voices has waned is that we no longer practice solitude and silence consistently, or in large doses. We don't pursue this kind of life, nor do we find ourselves in a quiet room all alone by accident. Our lives are noisy, distracted, and nearly always surrounded by people, real and virtual.

Sitting in silence all alone for the purpose of paying attention to what happens there is one of the most countercultural practices we could engage in. We don't need to arrive at hard and fast conclusions about which of these thoughts ought to be addressed from a theological lens or a psychological one. Evil exists in the world. I believe in the Accuser. And I suspect that those harsh and biting words trying to push me out of prayer are whispered in my ear by the enemy in ways that leverage the pain and trauma that I already hold. If you whisper a lie into someone's ear enough times, they begin to believe it. And now it is no longer a thought coming from the outside but rather one that comes from within. This, I think, is what happens when we are quiet and alone with the intention to pursue the presence of God and are suddenly present to both the normal distractions and the ones rooted in anger and envy and pride and lust. How do we sort out where all these thoughts are coming from? And what do we do about them?

For Evagrius, as for Saint Anthony before him, it felt therapeutic to externalize at least some of those thoughts by assigning them to demons so that he could fight them. He fought them with the Scriptures and developed a robust list of specific Scriptures to use against each of the eight thoughts emerging from the passions.[4]

Versions of Evagrius's system centered around eight thoughts (later reduced to seven deadly sins) continue to make their rounds through books and podcasts and trainings through the Enneagram tradition. This tradition says that personality (as a psychological category) is rooted in the reality that we tend to fall into a few patterns of thought. We live out of those patterns in ways that stick. And this often makes us feel stuck. The patterns become automatic, and we are driven by these underlying thoughts and the motivations that stem from them. The work of silence and solitude (and the contemplative prayer that we engage in there) constrains our awareness so that we can focus on what is happening right now in the present moment.

And in this moment we can do the work of sifting and sorting those thoughts.

After Evagrius came John Cassian, who was in many ways responsible for synthesizing the Egyptian monasticism of the East and bringing it west. He represents a later tradition of dealing with distracting thoughts in prayer. The later traditions recognized that perhaps Evagrius's direct approach to fighting the demons was for the more experienced monk. If you've been studying the Scriptures and meditating on the Psalms for years and have them on the tip of your tongue to wield against those taunting lies of the enemy—by all means, swing the sword.

But what about the rest of us? What about the beginners? What about the mom of young kids who is carving out twenty minutes of quiet during nap time with a tepid cup of tea in her hand trying to settle into the love of God?

Cassian and Evagrius agreed on a starting point: we have to learn to sift and sort. Some of the thoughts that come to us in the place of solitude and silence are from outside of us (from the world or the devil) and some are from within ourselves. But other thoughts that come to us in the place of solitude and silence are from God. We are, after all, there to meet with God. It shouldn't surprise us that he would draw our attention to one or two things from time to time. The practice and training in the constraint of this present moment is about sifting and sorting where the thoughts are coming from.

John Cassian uses the metaphor. He says that we have to become like "prudent money changers" sitting at a table. When you are a moneychanger, sometimes people try to hand you counterfeit coins. We have to learn the feel of authentic thoughts that we ought to stay present with and bring into conversation with God, and the feel of the thoughts that try to pull us out of that place of presence with God, which we might need to reject altogether.

Abba Moses said, "It's impossible for the mind not to be disturbed by thoughts, but it is possible for every earnest person either to accept or to reject them."[5] This process of sorting and sifting is a process of discernment. This takes practice. We cannot accomplish much by simply taking a retreat day a few times a year. Solitude and silence must become a part of our life. Only then can we learn through the practice of constraining our attention to the present moment how to discern where these thoughts are coming from. We grow in our ability to weigh the thoughts and the distractions, to toss some of them aside and to sit with others with a prayerful posture in God's presence. Some thoughts that come to us feel harsh, accusatory, biting. The ancient tradition would tell us to reject such a thought—confront it with Scripture, name it as a "lie," and toss it aside.

There can be some wisdom in this approach, but I also want to offer another posture. Some of these harsh, accusatory, and biting thoughts might be worth getting curious about. If we recognize that some of these distracting thoughts are rooted in the passions deep within us, we might wonder what they reveal about the wounded places in our lives. Sure, the demons might be wielding the power of those wounds. But Christ is the healer.

My own experience of shifting from "fighting the demons" to getting curious about what material they have at their disposal in the deep part of my being has turned out to be a different way of fighting. I'm still fighting, but my strategy has shifted.[6] I don't need to be afraid of what the enemy is pushing into my face as a source of distraction. I might be surprised by it, and I might be terrified by it. But something shifted for me when I began to fight in this new way.

Where is the enemy getting all this material? What part of me is handing this material over? What is the source of those thoughts, and how might God want to come into those places and offer healing? We'll come back to this posture of curiosity in chapter ten, "Formational Healing."

The practice of solitude and silence and the constraint of the present moment turns out to be preparatory work for a lot of what lies ahead, especially in relation to the practice of formational healing (see chap. 10). In short, when we are doing the work of sifting and sorting, we're doing the work of discernment.[7] Some of the thoughts that come to us when we commit to staying in the present moment and growing in awareness about what comes up are thoughts to be accepted, while some are to be rejected. We can grow in this practice as we continue to come to solitude and silence and do the work of sorting and sifting. And there are times when we have only the grace to just watch all the thoughts pass us by. Sometimes it is better not to engage in any of the thoughts at all. If the enemy wants to play tennis with you and hits you a burner, just don't return the serve. Let the ball bounce wherever it bounces. Game over![8]

If you keep showing up to this space and practicing the constraint of the present moment in silence and solitude, eventually you will see a warbler.

Seeing the Warbler

What does it look like to "find a warbler" in the practice of solitude and silence? Remember, the immediate goal of this way of life that we are pursuing—a life of constraint that, in faith, we believe will lead to freedom—is purity of heart. We are partnering with God to become free of the way the passions enslave us. The constraint is just a means to get to where we're going. And where we are going, once we're humbled by the weakness we discover in the fight against everything that is happening in the present moment, where years of patterned desires can flood us in an instant, is resting in the love of our Father.

God's love is found in participation. And what often keeps us from experiencing the love of God is our lack of participation. We're invited to step into the rain, but we don't make it rain. We show up to the park bench and look through the binoculars, but we can't make the warblers come. The constraint of the present moment is a hard constraint. We often, I think, give up too soon.

In the practice of solitude and silence we take seriously our role in drawing near to God with the faith that he will in turn draw near to us (Jas 4:8). And as we draw near to God and sort and sift through all the distractions and passions and desires and resistance in the midst of our lives, alongside the quiet place of God's presence, we feel the grace of God, who is there to help us. And then we rest in the surety that he is our Father and that he is caring for us even when what we find in the present moment is pain or grief or terror. Eventually, the training allows us to calm those thoughts, feel less distracted, discard the lies, and hold the truth in the presence of God.

There's a line in Cassian's *Conferences* that Merton, in one of his lectures to the Novitiates in 1963, zeros in on. Cassian is talking about contemplative prayer, which is where we're trying to get to with this training in solitude and silence. We're trying to simply *rest* in God's presence. This is the central nature of contemplative prayer. And Merton spends nearly twenty minutes with his students digesting the Latin of this ancient text. Why? Because it's about what happens when you see a warbler. Sometimes something actually does happen in that space of solitude and silence. And when it does, it's one hundred percent grace.

In this line, Cassian writes, "The mind, in the love of God, is untied and thrown back into God. Most familiarly, one now speaks to God as one's very own Father with a very intimate love."[9] Merton says that the image of being untied (we gain our freedom) and thrown back (passive release into God's care) means that we don't simply recognize God as the Father of everyone. Each of us recognizes that he's *my* Father. And the love that we share together is a *unique* love. It's the kind of love that two people have when they belong to one another.[10] The fruit of the asceticism—constraining and training our attention to the present moment—is humility. And through this humility we learn that God uniquely loves each of us.

He is *my* Father.

And in this place, we get a clear view of what is actually true of us. Even though we are full of all that chaos that we see when we're finally quiet enough to see it, we are beloved. We have to see through the chaos of the present moment in order to see the love within the present moment.

Elsewhere Merton describes this view of ourselves as "a clear unobstructed vision of the true state of affairs, an intuitive grasp of one's own inner reality. As anchored, or rather lost, in God through Christ."[11] And when we are anchored—or lost—in God, we are free. God has sent the Spirit of his Son into our hearts—the Spirit who calls out, "Abba, Father" (Gal 4:6).

The Freedom to Rest

Another word for what happens in this kind of freedom is what the early fathers called *quies. Quies* is a particular kind of rest in God. And living in this place—living *from* this place—in the world that we inhabit, is a prophetic act. Living from this place regularly makes for a prophetic life.

The kind of rest that the desert fathers spoke of was a spiritual rest. A quietness of heart. A freedom from striving and a freedom from needing to be something or someone particularly special or "anointed" or "favored" by others. It's the freedom to let your bathroom be what it is, or renovate if you want, but not because you have to. It's the kind of rest that one attains when one is truly standing in the grace of God in a way that puts aside all self-justification and ambition. It is a kind of rest that is able to set one's own self-importance in this world aside, not because one devalues oneself but precisely the opposite.

The rest that we find when we are *untied* and *thrown back* into the lap of our Father is a kind of rest that recognizes our extreme value to God. And this is enough. And once it is enough, we can do anything. Or absolutely nothing. Because in this place of *quies* we are free.

The beauty of living this way is that it is one of the most *prophetic* things we can do in the world. Imagine meeting someone who is no longer striving for the top. It doesn't mean they aren't working hard putting their shoulder into whatever they are doing. Nor does it mean that there are no late nights and early mornings and sleepless seasons when anxiety steals their rest. But they work at motherhood or fatherhood or teaching or pastoral ministry or any other kind of work without that hustle that seems like it's killing them. They labor instead with a sense of interior

spiritual ease. This is someone who is living in the freedom offered by the love of the Father while letting that love fuel the way
they live. This person is like a sheep who comes to a green pasture
and simply lies down rather than anxiously eating as much grass
as they can take in. "What kind of a sheep lies down in a green
pasture?" asks Dallas Willard. "A sheep that has eaten its fill already. If a sheep is in a green pasture and she's not full, she'll be
eating, not lying down."[12]

Can you imagine living in this way? How different would living
this way feel for you in the areas that you feel yourself striving?
For me, one of my greatest places of striving—where I have carried
some anxiety—has been in my need to be the "best" dad my girls
could have. And yet, something has shifted for me as I have leaned
into solitude and silence and found in that place a deeper sense of
the love of God. I still very much want to be a great dad to my girls.
But I also feel a freedom to just be myself, to allow my life to be
what it is, to settle into the fact that I am going to make mistakes—
something that was previously unsettling to me.

Imagine if our churches were filled with people living from a
place of rest, entirely sure of the love of God, not striving to "get
ahead" in ways that feel out of place in the world and not needing
to be anything other than who God is making them.

PRACTICING
SOLITUDE AND SILENCE

For Pastors and Leaders

If you are a pastor or a leader in a local church, beginning this journey
with solitude and silence might feel like a hard place to start. I'm glad
that more pastors are taking sabbath seriously, and I know many are

intentional about it. I suspect that practicing solitude and silence outside of your sabbath is going to be challenging, but I invite you to try to lean in to the work of solitude and silence on the other days of the week as well. Perhaps my perspective on this is driven by temperament and personality, but I also spend a lot of time with pastors in spiritual direction and my quick take is this: most pastors are not spending enough time alone.

It takes a tremendous amount of time alone as a leader to get clear about the place you are drawing from in ministry. We all know that Jesus regularly spent time praying by himself. Luke specifically says that Jesus did this *frequently*.

- ❖ Schedule in your calendar blocks of forty-five minutes each day over the next thirty days. This doesn't mean that you absolutely have to do it, but it will be there for you. I find that I need about forty-five minutes to find about twenty minutes of actual presence to God.
- ❖ Grab a couple of friends or colleagues (members of church staff or other pastors in your city) and invite them to lean into the practice of solitude with you over the next thirty days.
- ❖ Keep a journal of the thoughts that come up when you sit for twenty minutes of silent, contemplative prayer.
- ❖ Ask God to give you the grace to experience his unique love for you and for you to experience God as your very own Father.

For Small Groups

One of the most beautiful—and sometimes awkward—experiences is sitting in silence in a room full of people. While this isn't actually the same as solitude, practicing with others can be a way of training toward being able to do it alone. There is solidarity in a group. And yes, it can get a little awkward but it's okay—it's probably a little awkward for everyone. If you are working through this book in the context of a home group or community group that meets regularly, begin your time with a brief guided silence. Eight to ten minutes is a good amount of time to begin with. See www.orderofthecommonlife.org for resources.

❖ Gather regularly with a group of people to practice silence. Every time you gather as a group, just practice.

❖ Carve out some regular time within your personal schedule to practice solitude and silence. Encourage each member of the group to bring calendars to a group meeting. Help one another talk through the shape of your lives. When can you create space in your schedule for solitude and silence? It might be different for each person. The process of inviting people into your calendar and into the shape of your life can help you think about your life rhythms differently than you would by yourself.

❖ Set aside a thirty-day challenge where everyone in the group commits to some version of this practice of solitude (spending time alone) and silence (sitting quietly in God's presence).

❖ Pay attention to the thoughts that come up during your times of solitude and silence. Keep a journal and write down what you notice. What thoughts do you gravitate toward when you are alone and there are no distractions? What distractions come up when you sit quietly in a prayerful posture? Are there recurring thoughts? Write them down.

❖ Come together in your group meetings and share what you are noticing. *I notice I think a lot about the conversations I've had that day. I notice I get distracted by all the deadlines that await me. I notice that when I'm by myself, I feel more anxious.*

❖ Offer to pray for one another.

❖ Take a half-day retreat by yourself. It doesn't need to be fancy. We have a half-day retreat guide at www.orderofthecommonlife.org to give you some rails to run on.

For Parents

When is it even possible to have solitude and silence when you have children?

I know. I get it. We have four girls and it takes some creativity to make this happen. In the early years, when the girls were little, we tag-teamed. We did our best to help one another get the time needed. This meant that I woke up early and spent that first forty-five minutes of my day (with coffee) in an old red leather chair in our living room. My time of solitude and silence more often than not ended with a little one on my lap—and I wouldn't have it any other way. My girls all have memories of waking up with me in that chair, or the black one that followed, or the gray one that came after that.

Some of the training of solitude and silence that happens for kids happens passively as they watch us make room for it. If your kid wakes up each morning and sees you with eyes closed taking some deep breaths, they might not know that you are fighting the devil, or anxiety, or a deep desire for a new job—but you can tell them about it someday. My girls are getting old enough for me to let them in on some of what those struggles were about in those years. I've been able to talk with them about what it felt like to have them "interrupt" me by coming to sit on my lap. I've been able to share with them the ways that God loved me through those moments and how I learned to pray for them during this time.

The temptation for me in the beginning of practicing solitude and silence—and more specifically the contemplative prayer that I was trying to carve out room for—has always been to just grab a book and read during that time. I love to read. And what I now know is that oftentimes my reach for a book is really just another form of distraction. The truth is that after ten years of practicing solitude and silence I still sometimes struggle with how much is going on inside my head and heart. I've learned that grabbing a book means I don't actually have to constrain myself to the present moment—but then I'm no longer practicing silence, am I? Reading is lovely. It's just not what this practice is about.

❖ Find a few days in your week when you can carve out forty-five minutes to practice being alone in God's presence without a book or music or anything else.

❖ Make it a point to communicate to your kids what you're doing. *Mommy's going to have some solitude and silence.*

❖ As much as possible, try not to view this time as "getting away" but rather as "coming toward." We're approaching a holy space.

❖ Try out some age-appropriate solitude and silence times for your kids. In our house we simply called this "alone time." It doesn't need to be a prayer time for kids. Just sowing seeds of solitude throughout their childhood can pay off in the long run.

I think "time out" as a form of punishment needs to disappear. Being alone in one's big emotions is not a good idea—either for the emotions or for the practice of being alone. Make alone time a positive experience rather than a form of punishment.

Tell your kids often about the love of God. For you and for them.

CHAPTER SIX

SIMPLICITY

CHOOSING THE CONSTRAINT OF
OUR ATTENTION

The Freedom to See

Be attentive to yourself, that is, observe yourself carefully from every

side. Lest the eye of your soul be sleepless to guard yourself. You walk

in the midst of snares. Hidden traps have been set by the enemy in

many places. Therefore observe everything, "that you may be saved

like a gazelle from traps and like a bird from snares" (Prov. 6.5).

BASIL OF CAESAREA

We hit peak minimalism sometime just before the Covid-19 pandemic. The lifestyle of living with less and being happy with what you have reached its height of popularity. Decluttering your closet, getting rid of books that you haven't touched in years—both sparked by Marie Kondo's bestselling book and accompanying Netflix special—and even buying a "less-smart"

phone as an act of "digital minimalism,"[1] all made their rounds through middle-class America.

I've watched it all unfold. I've participated.

This chapter on simplicity is not a chapter on minimalism.

The minimalism movement is about self-actualization, or what postmodern philosopher Michel Foucault might call a "technology of the self." A technology of the self is individuals acting *upon* themselves for the sake of becoming or acquiring something like wisdom or virtue or perfection. Anything we do with ourselves can work this way—but *how* it works boils down to our intentions.

Minimalism is a predominately upper-middle-class Instagram-mable phenomenon that leads people to own only clothing that "sparks joy" and centers around the concept of decluttering one's possessions. The intention of minimalism is being attentive to oneself and one's surroundings for the sake of one's own self.

Simplicity, at least the kind that I am guiding us toward, is rooted in historic asceticism with the goal of focusing our attention so that we might see clearly. It is in line with Saint Basil's idea that we are to be attentive to ourselves not for the sake of ourselves but for the sake of our life as it is before God.[2] The object of our ultimate attention is God's invitation to a loving relationship that leads to union with God. We are not pursuing simplicity for the sake of becoming someone who lives simply. We are pursuing simplicity so that we might see more clearly the love and the work of God in our lives.

The practice of the constraint of our attention is not meant to feel like a task to pursue or a job to perform. Perhaps it will lead you to give some attention to your relationship with clothing and to clean out your closet. Or you might begin to reimagine your relationship with food and eating after much prayer and reflection. You may even consider what it means for you, as a follower of Jesus, that we live in a culture that is hellbent on the accumulation of wealth. But you may not feel an invitation from the Spirit to do anything at all.

If you do feel like making some changes in your life, it will do no good if this new way of life carries with it a sense of obligation. As with any practice of constraint, the invitation is to cultivate a presence to God—and more specifically, to cultivate presence to God so that we might *see* the love of God and his invitations to us from within that loving gaze. We learn how to love others primarily by seeing and by watching the way that God loves us. The question is not whether or not God loves us. This, I hope, can become settled for you in the practice of solitude and silence. The question to consider is whether or not our lives are clear enough of distraction to be present and *see* the way that God is loving us.

Is there anything at all, in the very tangible everyday living of our life, that is simply obstructing our view of God's love for us? Constraining or focusing our *attention* is a means of developing the "keenest of *sight* like the gazelle," as Saint Basil said. We do this so that we will not be taken captive by the enemy and so that we might "keep the *gaze* of our soul unrestricted."[3] The gaze is toward God and God's love for us and those around us.

Simplicity as a form of training and as a spiritual discipline is about becoming free from the complexity of relationship that we have with things that might be restricting our gaze toward God. Are we using these things as self-medication of the unhealed passions? If we remove the medicine, the sickness becomes more visible, and we may more fully participate in God's healing of us.

There are infinite ways that we can self-medicate and distract ourselves. There are so many things that might be obstructing our view. But historically Christians have focused their training practice and attention on food, clothing, and possessions. If we train our attention in these everyday areas, we can learn to see how adept we are at self-medicating the unhealed passions. It's easy for us to keep envy and lust hidden from our view because these passions are primarily expressed through emotions—and emotions are quite easy to dull. Pursuing simplicity in our relationship to food, clothing, and possessions is just a place to begin. Once we learn how we are using these to manage our unhealed passions, we can apply this insight to other areas.[4]

The Constraint of Attention

Keep yourselves from idols.

John the Evangelist, 1 John 5:21

The journey toward freedom does not happen only in "spiritual" activities. The Christian life is more than just the pursuit of believing the right things, praying the right ways, and serving in a local church.

Believe. Pray. Serve. Much of the Christian life has been centered on this in the West. But the life of following Jesus happens with tangible things in our hands, in our homes, and with our bodies. Most of our discipleship to Jesus is embedded in the everyday activities of our lives.

The freedom we seek in our interior space with God cannot be divorced from the everyday engagement of our lives. This reality of "everyday engagement" will almost always include the *people* in our life (see chap. 10).

The traffic between what happens interiorly in our soul and the unconsidered and ingrained routines we engage in goes both ways. Our inner desires compel us to act in the world in certain ways. We develop habits. Those habits form us and become entrenched in behaviors that reinforce the unhealed passions that are already very much at work. The vainglory just below the surface compels us to pick up our phone for the 305th time today to scroll the feed. Or maybe it's not vainglory. Maybe it's just acedia or boredom. But this act of scrolling then feeds back into that interior desire that drove us to this habit in the first place. It's a two-way road. Our internal world—that little steam factory of passions—compels us outward to act in the world in ordinary ways—eating, drinking, scrolling. And those ordinary behaviors in the everyday habits of our life do a number on our interior life. They keep us entrenched in the behavior.

And this is why we are often not operating in freedom even when we think we are.

One of the greatest dangers of the contemplative tradition—and the ascetic practices that have always been a part of the tradition—is the temptation to make the spiritual life only about what happens interiorly while disregarding the material world we live in. The early practitioners of constraint recognized the two-way traffic, and they tried to put a stop to it simply by cutting off engagement from the everyday world. In the early years of the monastic tradition there was still at work a false belief about the material world. Simply put, they believed the material world is bad and the spiritual world is good.

This way of thinking fueled the worst kinds of abuse. The constraints on the body multiplied in these early communities because they thought the body was part of the physical/material world and therefore was the cause of all the bad things happening in the soul. These early errors rested on a disregard for the material world: *If we conquer the material world (our bodies), then our souls will be free to love and serve God.* Or so they thought.

Abstaining from food became a contest. Men lived for years on top of pillars as acts of radical asceticism. There are ridiculous stories about little worms feeding on the flesh of men who said to the worms, "Eat what God has given you." They kept track of how many years it had been since they had seen a woman. Of course, we can now see how misguided all of this is.

Much of the falsehood of this belief eventually got worked out. But it took some time. This way of "training the body" was much more influenced by the surrounding cultural philosophies than it was by a robust Christian theology. We should be gracious in our reading of these early formational efforts simply because there was little established theology when these men and women were trying to figure out what it meant to become "all flame." These early monastic communities were doing their best while all the theology was still being sorted. It took years of practice before Christian asceticism became truly Christian, embodied in the right way and rooted in the *incarnational* life of a God who made the human with a body that is *good*. Asceticism and constraint didn't disappear, but the fringe practices *against* the body began to fade away. The war against the body went away and eventually practitioners began to understand that the body and its limits are part of the way that God does his work in us. We follow a God who took on a body, died with a body, and has a resurrected body even now.

The core instinct of these early experiments in Christian asceticism, which got lost in a cultural context where the physical world was "bad" and the spiritual world was "good," is that the primary work of the spiritual life is *attachment to God*. This they got right.

The spiritual life is about attachment to God. It's about focusing our attention on the love of God.[5] This attachment and attention to God's love is a central feature of contemplative spirituality. The love of God is the only thing that empowers real change in our lives. This is why the apostle Paul prays for the Ephesians that they might be "rooted and grounded in love." It's the love of God in Christ that "strengthens the inner person with power" (Eph 3:15-19).

This attention to the love of God is what those early contemplatives practicing asceticism were pursuing. They were trying to become unattached to the "things of this world"—the reliance on food and drink and riches—such that they might become attached to God alone. They were moving the focus of their attention away from the things that dull the spiritual senses and toward the fullness of God who dwelled in their own hearts. Those early practitioners were simply training their lives toward having more room for what is real in their lives. They learned to let go of everything that did not serve them in their turn toward God's love.

The Christian tradition is peppered with exhortations about wealth and riches, eating too much, getting caught up in a focus on outward appearance—and the ways that all of these can distract us from what is real and in need of attention in our inner life with God. These things can fill up our soul to such a degree that there is no room to be attentive to what God has placed within us: a desire for God so strong that it is unquenchable with anything else.

And this unquenchable desire for God serves a higher purpose. As members of Christ's body in the world, we are meant to be filled with the love of God such that we might give to the world the life of God, which is being birthed through the Spirit, who has made a home inside of us.

By constraining our attention, at least for a season of reflection (and possibly, for some, even longer), on these basic areas of our everyday lives, we begin to ask deeper questions that we may not otherwise ask: Is there anything in my life that is getting in the way? Is there anything that is dulling my desire to be filled with God's very own self? Is there anything blocking my view of God's love? We turn our attention to these three areas with curiosity about what complexity and distraction and self-medication they bring into our life. I suspect that not every one of these areas will feel relevant to you, but I am almost certain that at least one of them will.

In the end, what comes to us as a gift through the constraint of our attention is the eyes to see what is really happening with our unhealed passions. And there we can also see the deeper invitations of God's love.

The Practice of Simplicity

Food. One story from the desert fathers goes like this: "Once two brothers went to visit an old man. It was not the old man's habit, however, to eat every day. When he saw the brothers, he welcomed them with joy, and said: 'Fasting has its own reward, but if you eat for the sake of love, you satisfy two commandments, for you give up your own will and also fulfill the commandment to refresh others.'"[6]

Most historic practices of asceticism related to food have centered on fasting. I think fasting is one of the most important things we can do to help us be attentive to what is happening in deeper places. A regular practice of welcoming the weakness that fasting can bring helps train us toward a greater reliance on God and what God can provide. We're reminded of our very real dependence on God when we feel it in our bodies. When paired with deeper questions of reflection in prayer and an invitation for God to speak to us, fasting is one of the most accessible practices of constraint that nearly everyone without a medical condition that prevents it should practice.

The practice of fasting is quite simple: (1) Refrain from food for a specified period of time. Skip one meal. Skip two. Or try twenty-four hours with just water.[7] (2) During and after your fast ask God one question: "Is there anything you'd like to say to me during this time?"

Fasting by itself will not change one thing about you. Fasting can make visible your interior world, which will create a context for deeper engagement with the love of God. If, in fasting, you see that there are unhealed passions at work that show up in your relationship with food—now we're getting to what fasting is meant to do. Fasting is a tool to help us be attentive to the deeper things. In the same way that the practice of sabbath was not the goal of the Sabbath—at least as Jesus understood it (Mk 2:27)—the practice of fasting is useless unless we understand that it is meant to do something *for* us.

Even beyond fasting, there is an even more basic question: What is my relationship with food and drink? What is happening in my life that works its way out in my relationship with food? Let me offer a few examples of how one's relationship with food can be complex and how the complexity of that relationship might be rooted in an unhealed passion standing in the way of a deeper awareness of the inner work that God wants to attend to.

I know a woman who has had an awareness of food addiction in her life for as long as she can remember. She's been a follower of Jesus her whole life, and in her midtwenties she became aware of the fact that she often ran to food when she felt deep emotions and anxiety. She noticed that her relationship with food was more complex than she wanted it to be. And it was taking up room—lots of room—in her mind. She would think about food all the time. She would try to talk with people about it but, because she was not overweight, whatever struggle she had with food seemed so trite. How could someone so thin think that she had a food addiction?

For nearly twenty years this woman had a deep awareness that her relationship with food, particularly with sugar, was dulling her emotions, numbing her to the emotions of others, and impacting her ability to love fully and more fully receive love. In her mid-forties she began to learn more about how sugar had hijacked her brain, and as she began to constrain this particular part of her relationship with food—at the invitation of God in prayer and in spiritual direction—something radical began to shift for her. She gained access to what was really going on at some deeper levels. She became present to the unhealed passions of pride, which were manifesting as shame, and God began to heal her of some deep insecurities. He did it through exposing the unhealed passions and demonstrating to her that even in the most vulnerable place of shame, especially in that place, God was right there loving her.

In a recent conversation among a cohort of spiritual friends[8] where we spent some time asking questions about our relationship with food (among other things), a man in his late twenties reflected to the group some of what he was noticing about this area of his life. He told about how he ate food he didn't like simply because it was cheap. And it wasn't that he didn't have money to buy food he wanted. He wanted to buy food that was good for his body—fresh fruits and vegetables—but when he went to the grocery store there was something happening below the surface that prevented him from doing what he wanted to do. There was a voice telling him that healthy food is expensive and you should not spend money on healthy food. And so he bought the cheapest food that he could find, even though he had the money to buy the food he wanted.

This man's relationship with food revealed that there was something wounded in his relationship with money. He grew up poor, and the place in his life that he most remembers being poor is in the food that he ate. Whenever he gets nice food, he saves it rather than eating it because there is something at work in him that resists enjoying good food simply because healthy food costs more money than unhealthy food.

In the first story, the focus of attention on the complexity of relationship with food turned into an invitation toward fasting. The woman cut out sugar and found that she had relied on sugar to mask all kinds of emotions. She also experienced more of the love of God, not because God loved her more because of her fasting but because she could now see that even in this place of weakness, which she had spent years covering up, God was right there.

In the second story, the focus of attention on the complexity of relationship with food ultimately turned into an invitation toward feasting. He began to spend money on food he actually desired and he found more of the experience of God's love in the gift of that good food. He felt a deep invitation toward celebration and joy in a place that he previously was not allowing himself the freedom to experience.

Neither individual experienced freedom from unhealed passions before giving this area the focus and constraint of attention. But for both, a simple turn of attention, held in prayer, talked about in community, revealed unhealed passions below the surface that were leaking out in a complex relationship with food.

- As I pay attention to what I eat and drink, how would I describe my relationship with food?
- What rhythms or rituals do I experience with food, such as periods of fasting and feasting?
- What do I sense God inviting me to try as I turn my attention to my relationship with food?

Clothing. An ancient proverb says, "The cowl does not make the monk." A *cowl* is a long cloak with a hood worn by monks. The simplest interpretation of this popular ancient proverb is the reality that the external appearance of a monk or nun is not what directs their life toward God. You cannot simply put on a monk's habit and become a monk. And yet nearly every historic community living under a rule of life since the beginning of the church has had something to say about clothing. Much of our modern-day conversation around rule of life has not fostered, to my knowledge, a conversation around our clothing.[9] John Cassian, also called John the Ascetic, begins his *Institutes* not with a discussion of prayer or fasting nor with an exhortation about solitude or contemplation. He opens with a comment on what sort of clothing a community should adopt: "As we are going to speak of the customs and rules of the monasteries, how by God's grace can we better begin than with the actual dress of the monks, for we shall then be able to expound in due course their interior life when we have set them out."[10]

Nearly every rule of life within this tradition talks about clothing. From Benedict to Saint Francis, from Augustine to Saint Ignatius—everyone has something to say about the role of one's attire. If we give it only a moment of thought, it seems absurd: robes, belts, shoes, hats. There is even discussion about how long one's sleeves should be.

But if we suspend judgment and give these instructions about clothing a little more of our attention, we might discover that there is something here, perhaps a principle that we can learn something from. These are the same people, after all, who have given us almost *all* of our theology, ways of praying, and liturgies. Nearly all of what we believe about following Jesus has its roots in these early monastic communities. Our forms of prayer were birthed by the same men and women who took the time to think about their clothing.

I suspect that you did not pick up this book because you have ever thought about monasticism or John Cassian or what monks wore in the fourth century. I have no interest in telling you what you should or shouldn't wear, though I have come to think that perhaps we might consider giving it at least a little of our attention, given how full most of our closets are and the impact of "fast fashion" on the poor of the world.

The history of the wardrobe of monks and nuns is fascinating. The early practitioners of the rule of life and constraint were the first Christians to give clothing any significant meaning. In their world clothing became symbolic. It served as a constant reminder, both within the community and to the external world, that they were up to something different. The short sleeves of a linen tunic, in a world where long sleeves were sought out as a sign of elegance, reminded the brothers that they had, as Cassian describes, "cut off the deeds and works of this world." The small hood, which the monks wore day and night, was there that "they may constantly be moved to preserve the simplicity and innocence of little children by imitating their actual dress."[11] The tunics, the chords of rope beneath the armpits and around the waist, and their sandals (or the decision to go without shoes altogether)—everything was done to reinforce, to habituate, the community toward the way of life that they were trying to embody.

What can we take from this that could be helpful? Very simply: What is your relationship with your wardrobe?

Not all of our clothes need to take on meaning. I'm not interested in dressing like a monk, though I did pair down my wardrobe when I noticed, about a decade ago, that I had an odd relationship with being "in style." For some reason in my early years of adulthood I had an incessant need to look a particular way. So I have been wearing what amounts to a uniform for the past ten years. It has felt like freedom to me. This doesn't mean the same will be true for you, but it is part of my story.

I also know some Anglican clergy who have given their wardrobe some thought. My Anglican friends who are priests have considered the significance of their clothes because when they wear their priestly collar, people seem to open up to them. This, for them, has been meaningful.

In the same way we looked at the everyday activity of eating and what complexities exist in our relationship with food, let's consider the complexities related to clothing. Perhaps you have a closet full of clothes that you never wear. This practice of constraint invites you to give this area of your life some attention.

Would you be willing, for a season, to constrain your attention to your relationship with clothing to get curious about whether you have any disordered attachment related to what you wear? Or what brand you wear? Or what others are wearing? Are you spending more money than you have in order to find just the right look?

Maybe none of these is remotely connected to your experience of clothing. But here's another angle to consider. Consider your choice of clothing as it relates to gaining freedom to love others with your choice of clothing brands. So much of our fast-fashion clothing is sewn and produced by modern-day slaves. Many of the world's most famous brands regularly face accusations of profiting from slave labor.[12] If my own need to stay in fashion or find a "good deal" undermines my commitment to fair and just treatment of others, then I am not operating in a freedom to love. The clothing industry is a complex system with multiple supply chains. It can be challenging to choose clothing from companies who are turned toward justice. But those companies do exist. And there are choices. It will probably mean being less "in fashion" or "on brand" and will also probably mean that we own less clothing. The true cost of clothing when you include fair labor wages means that fair-wage clothing is more expensive.

This is just one example of how turning our attention toward clothing might cause some practical and formational implications to bubble up in our lives.

- As I pay attention to my clothing, what do I notice about my relationship with my wardrobe?
- What resistance do I notice?
- What might I sense God inviting me to try as I turn my attention in this direction?

Possessions and wealth. Jesus said to the rich man, "If you wish to be perfect, go, sell your possessions, and give the money to the poor, and you will have treasure in heaven; then come, follow me." Poverty and wealth are both terrible burdens. The burdens of poverty are well documented and observable. We know that the poor are suffering. And we know that the inequalities between the rich and poor are growing at rates that are unsustainable.

What is less visible is the burden—the very real but hidden burden—of great wealth. If you are reading this book, you are likely wealthy, at least by global standards. Have you ever considered your relationship to possessions and wealth as complex or burdensome?

Within the contemplative and ascetic traditions of religious orders, nearly every community, whether scattered like the Jesuits or cloistered like the Cistercians, has negotiated a relationship with wealth and possessions. Saint Francis advocated radical poverty in solidarity with the poor. Those following the Rule of Benedict took vows of individual poverty but lived in communities that often accumulated a great deal of resources through the acquisition of land. No one living in a monastery is experiencing poverty in any real way. Everything is provided. Saint Ignatius of Loyola taught that we should maintain a posture of neutrality regarding wealth and possessions: "We should not prefer health to sickness, riches to poverty, honor to dishonor, a long life to a short life. . . . Our one desire and choice should be what is more conducive to the end for which we are created."[13]

The hidden burden of wealth is one that is very difficult to uncover. It was easy for Jesus to uncover the burden for the rich younger rule by getting right to the heart of the matter. Jesus was, with one statement, able to reveal to the man that his love for his wealth and possessions was the only thing that stood in the way of him getting exactly what he wanted. What he truly desired at some deep and unseen place, revealed by the kinds of questions he was asking of Jesus, was to inherit something far different than he had already inherited. He wanted God and the things that God had promised. And yet, he was not free to get what he wanted because he had already acquired most of what he thought he wanted and had now taken too much comfort in them. Jesus' very simple approach was this: "Give them up."

When the early desert fathers went out into the desert, they took this at face value. Monastic literature emphasizes the need to make a decisive break with the temptation toward the accumulation of wealth and possessions. The benefit that this action bestowed on the poor was not the main concern, though the poor were often recipients of the wealth that these men and women discarded. They found their freedom through a radical turn away from the attention that their wealth and possessions had accumulated and toward a singular attention to the possibility that they could become full of God's transforming love.

The greatest concern was the need to "rid oneself of the burden of worldly possessions."[14] What they were paying attention to is true of all of us: we have an inordinate desire to possess things. What we possess and how much we possess is not the main issue that this tradition of constraint is concerned with. The vow of poverty in many of the monastic traditions is just the means to get at what lies underneath. Look at how quickly the very thought of giving up all his possessions caused the rich young man's previously hidden attachment to these possessions to surface. He didn't even have to actually give anything up to learn something that he didn't previously know; he needed his wealth. Jesus' question helped turn his attention to this fact. It was getting in the way of the eternal life he was seeking.

The struggle with getting at this hidden burden and over-attachment to wealth and possessions is that we can go right along living our wealthy life without anyone ever challenging it. There really is much more to say about wealth and possessions and the complexity of the relationship we might have with what we own and how much attention our possessions or the pursuit of riches occupies in our lives. Consider these questions in prayer and conversation with others:

- How is my relationship to wealth and possessions helping or hindering me in following the invitations of Jesus?
- What possessions do I desire? What might be behind this desire? Is this a healed desire or an unhealed passion?
- How might God be inviting me to simplify my relationship with the pursuit of wealth and possessions?

The Freedom to See

This journey toward increasing our attention toward simplifying our relationship with the most basic things in our life—the food we eat, the clothes we wear, and the possessions and wealth we accumulate—is not something we can do once and just be done with it. These are all necessary parts of our life. We can't eradicate our relationship with these things—they will always be there. And more than likely we will move in and out of seasons of complexity and simplicity. Our goal in the practice of constraint is simply to pay attention and nurture the ongoing work of seeing what we could not see before.

What we will likely discover—and what I have certainly discovered in my own practice—is that excessive complexity in one of these areas might reveal an array of interdependent desires and unhealed passions in other areas. One of the things at work in me, for as long as I can remember, is a fear of running out of money. This fear birthed overwork—both physical and mental—in my early adult years. I'm still asking God for healing. We might find that our anxieties about our investment portfolio are rooted in some of the same experiences (wounds, trauma, passions) that also impact our ability to connect deeply in intimacy with another or to believe that our relationships are secure. Or we might find that a season of abstinence from those after-work drinks help us get in touch with a fairly prevalent anxiety about our work or our marriage. Fasting from those evening cocktails might just help us realize, "Wow, without those drinks, my mind is pretty preoccupied." The constraint has helped us see something that we could not see before.

The practice of asceticism in these basic areas is so powerful because these are the places that so easily can hide what we might only be able to see through some of this deeper paying-attention work. Again, if you find that there are ways you are using food and drink, wealth and possessions, or you are really caught in a trap of some sort around clothing, there doesn't need to be any shame.

But there is an opportunity to feel humbled by it. Seeing this humility is simply part of the work of spiritual formation. The next step is to bring what you can now see into prayer and into a safe and loving community. The practice of prayer is nurtured through silence and solitude (see chap. 5). And bringing what we see into a loving community is found in the practice of faults and affirmations (see chap. 9).

There are a host of things that can distract us from the love of God and what God is tending to in our lives. Every one of these distractions comes to us through our bodies. And some of these become like the idols that John warned us about at the end of his first letter (1 Jn 5:21).

What the early practitioners of constraint got right was that this journey toward becoming "all flame" and pursuing union with God requires preparation and attention. It requires training. We have to remove some things that bring us comfort in order to discover ways that we might be covering over deeper desires for God.

Perhaps we have grown to love what God has made more than we love God himself. Of course, what God has made is a gift. But the gifts of God are meant to lead us toward God, not away from God. And sometimes we enjoy the gifts of God in ways that do not lead us toward God. Sometimes the gifts become the very things distracting us from God's love.

This preparation work that leads us toward union with God is not just something we can tack onto the front side of prayer. It's not a fifteen-minute pre-prayer technique of breathing or centering or slowing down. This might be a great place to begin. But what the men and women who gave us the monastic movement discovered is that this participatory work of preparation takes a lifetime of bodily engagement and experimentation. It's one's whole life leaning in one direction alongside others who are also leaning in that direction. The environment of our physical lives actually matters—our patterns of consumption, of eating and drinking and buying; the focus of our attention and what we do with our bodies; the environment that we build up around ourselves. Finding freedom through constraint is a process of attentiveness to some of the things that we perhaps have never considered as part of our spiritual formation.

And this is often a very slow process. And we should let it be slow. As Benedictine monk Columba Stewart says: "The gradual reorientation of the human person towards the reality of God . . . is what asceticism is all about."[15] If the early practitioners of constraints went a little too far in the importance they placed on the constraints of external and material things for the Christian life—such as austerity in food and clothing—the modern-day Christian is at risk of placing far too little importance on such constraints. We have perhaps grown accustomed to having too much.

PRACTICING
SIMPLICITY

For Pastors and Leaders

If you are a pastor or a leader in a local church, you might be tempted to skip this section. Food and clothing and possessions are probably not at the top of your list to preach on this year. These three topics in particular could very easily be misunderstood if talked about from the pulpit. I don't recommend preaching about food or clothing, but we need to hear pastors preach regularly about wealth and possessions.

As with all of these commitments, I encourage you to begin in your own life. Take an assessment of how some unhealed passions might be impacting the way you eat and drink, or the clothing you choose, or the way you accumulate wealth and possessions.

❖ Set aside some time in the next couple of weeks to consider each of these areas.

❖ Choose a way of fasting from food or alcohol or even sugary drinks like soda. Pay attention during this fasting period to what surfaces for you. Ask God to speak to you and give you eyes to see what God might reveal to you during this time.

❖ Grab a couple of friends or colleagues (on the church staff or other pastors in your city) and invite them to lean into the practice of fasting and get curious with one another about your relationship with food.

❖ Do you notice any unhealed passions in the area of clothing, wealth, or possessions? Are you experiencing any anxieties related to personal finances or your retirement portfolio? Spend some time talking with God in prayer about these things. Ask God to speak to you about what passions might be a work in this area. Talk with some trusted friends about what you notice.

❖ If you are in a tradition where you have the opportunity to wear a collar: What is your relationship with the practice of wearing a collar? Do you wear it outside of worship or only when you are "on duty"? Is there any invitation for you in this area?

For Small Groups

The areas of food, clothing, and possessions make for great conversation in a small group setting. Set aside a separate evening of conversation for each of these topics. Leading up to each conversation, have each person in the group spend the preceding week reflecting on that particular area of their life. This may be the first conversation that you are a part of around food and fasting, clothing, and the cultural force toward the accumulation of wealth.

Here are some other ideas:

❖ Pick a day of the week to fast together. Some might choose to fast from food or alcohol or coffee. Encourage each person to keep a journal about what they notice.

❖ Host an open and honest conversation where people in your group are able to share their financial struggles. Sometimes our relationship with wealth and possessions is primarily happening in our thoughts and is hard for others to see based on external realities.

❖ Support one another in divesting from possessions that take up too much room in your mind. Is there anything that you are obsessing over in a way that reveals some unhealthy attachment to possessions? What support do you need to begin removing some things in order to free up physical, mental, or emotional space to find a deeper attentiveness to God's work?

❖ Pay attention to the thoughts that come up as you focus your attention on each of these areas. Keep a journal and write down what you notice.

❖ Come together in your group meetings and share what you are noticing. *I notice that I eat a lot more when I'm feeling anxious. I wonder sometimes if I drink too often. I compare my clothing style to others a lot—I'm not sure why it's so important to me.* Whatever those thoughts are, write them down and share them with the group.

❖ Offer to pray for one another.

For Parents

Conversations around simplicity and the complex relationships we have with food, clothing, and possessions are some of the more challenging ones to think about in the life of a family. This conversation is not necessarily one that we can have with our kids in a way that is straightforward, unless of course there is a serious problem that emerges, such as an unhealthy or dangerous relationship with food, an addiction to shopping, or a tremendous fear around money.

Apart from these more extreme examples, most of our work as parents will be to help our children become aware, in age-appropriate ways, of the unhealthy attachments that might be emerging in their life.

Simply paying attention to the cultural messages that push unhealthy views of these things can bring opportunities for ongoing conversations.

Cultural messages around food and diet can quickly turn to internalized messages about body image for both girls and boys. Being overly restrictive or controlling over food choices can easily backfire. Providing a vision for a positive relationship with food is becoming more important as food-related diseases like childhood diabetes become health concerns. It's easier than ever to self-medicate with food that has been scientifically designed for addiction.

Similarly, there is nothing wrong with the desire to be *fashionable*, but sometimes this can turn into an obsession to fit in or have just the right look. The external practices don't need to drive our conversation with our kids. But having the eyes to see how these areas might reveal what is happening internally is one way to bring the practice of simplicity into age-appropriate conversations with our children.

Finally, we can steward conversations by noticing where we ourselves have placed an outsized emphasis on these areas. As you work your way through some of the questions this chapter brings up, consider sharing with your children what you notice about your own relationship with food, clothing, and wealth and possessions. Is there anything that God is inviting you to change in any of these areas of your life? Lean into those conversations in prayer, in spiritual friendship, and perhaps in spiritual direction. And, when you are ready, share some of your process with your children, as always in ways that are appropriate to their maturity.

CHAPTER SEVEN

MARRIAGE and CELIBACY

CHOOSING THE CONSTRAINT OF LOVE

The Freedom to Love

The vocation of the Christian is to die.

FATHER JOHN BEHR

*Unless a kernel of wheat falls to the ground and dies, it
remains only a single seed. But if it dies, it produces many
seeds. Anyone who loves their life will lose it, while anyone who
hates their life in this world will keep it for eternal life.*

JESUS

The primary reality of disciples of Jesus is death and resurrection. This is the guiding narrative of our life in Jesus.
Our baptism symbolizes this reality as we go into the watery grave and come out into resurrection life. We are reminded of this reality and we take it into our body in the Eucharist. We meditate

and preach on this truth throughout the Scriptures, where we are consistently reminded that the old human we once were has died and that we have been transformed into a new human (2 Cor 5:17), that the unhealed passions and desires have been crucified alongside Christ already (Gal 5:24-25), and yet we are to continue in the work of daily taking up our cross (of death) and following Christ into new resurrection life.

Jesus sums all of this up with a symbolic metaphor. He gives us an image of a grain of wheat falling to the ground, being buried, and then emerging from that death in a way that multiplies. Many seeds come from one seed. He is, of course, making reference to his own impending death and the "many seeds" (you and I and all the others) that will come from the grain of wheat that is his life being buried in a tomb. But he isn't only saying something about his life and how he is living. He is inviting us, as always, to model our way of life after his own. Death is at work in you and me and, as a result, life is at work in others. At least this is how the apostle Paul understood it (2 Cor 4:10-12).

Jesus invites us to follow him into the slow process of losing our life. And in doing so, we learn how to love in the way that he loved. He invites us to learn what he has learned—that the greatest way to show love for another is to die for their sake (Jn 15:13).

The most basic calling for the Christian is to *die*. The journey of humility is another name for this. And in our up-and-to-the-right world this is a difficult guiding story to keep at the center. Most of our church experience shapes us for the opposite. *Christianity Today*'s Mike Cosper and Russell Moore noted this on a bonus episode of the podcast *The Rise and Fall of Mars Hill*: "The whole purpose of the gathering of the church is to prepare people with their encounters with death. And, I think about this constantly in terms of how everything we do with our church gatherings runs in the opposite direction—it's all in the direction of triumphalism . . . of how great life can be. . . . I just wonder what role the whole *memento mori* thing has to play in the journey of the church?"[1]

Memento mori is a Latin phrase meaning "remember that you have to die." It's often associated with chapter four of Saint Benedict's Rule where he says, "Day by day remind yourself that you are going to die." Benedict is referring here to our actual death. The end-of-life death that awaits us all. But the spiritual formation tradition—particularly the one carved out for us by the desert fathers and mothers—invites us toward another kind of death: a *death of the self* that marks out a way toward the kind of love that Christ models. The paths of marriage and celibacy are both tangible reminders and means of the ongoing invitation to learn how to love. The church has historically understood both marriage and celibacy as forms of martyrdom because they function as "containers" that hold the process of giving up one's life, in various degrees, for the sake of another.

A Kind of Death

In the first few centuries of the church the path toward death for the sake of Jesus was a very real option. The idea that one might die for the sake of others became a part of the narrative of what it meant to follow the way of Jesus. Christians faced tremendous persecution under multiple Roman emperors. The age of the martyrs was a period where men and women bore witness to Christ through their death. They bore witness to the significance and meaning of Christ's death and resurrection by refusing to renounce their faith. They demonstrated for their pagan neighbors that as Christians they had already in some sense died with Christ and were even now living resurrected lives—or at least some version of a life that was headed toward resurrection. For the martyr dying meant union with God.

When Constantine became emperor, Christianity was folded into the life of the Roman Empire, and the persecutions and martyrdom of Christians came to a halt. There was no longer any real threat of death for Christians. And what it meant to "give away one's life for the sake of others" was slowly reimagined.

Emerging from this historic moment were two paths where the tradition and spiritual significance of martyrdom began to be reproduced. Many of the spiritual realities that were tied to martyrdom began to shift within preaching and practice toward new ways to bear witness. They were imagining new ways to "die." You could either learn how to die, and thus learn how to love, in marriage, or you could do so in a life of celibacy, generally alongside others who had also chosen this path (in a monastery). Marriage and celibacy became the two options for bearing witness through "death." Put less dramatically, one could learn that the greatest act of love is to give up one's life for the sake of others within the constraints provided in a lifelong commitment to loving one person uniquely. Or one could learn the same lesson through the constraints provided by a lifelong commitment to learning how to love a community of people, all of whom were devoting their lives to loving God as one would love a spouse.

The married person lived into the reality of their marriage as a demonstration of Christ and the church (Eph 5). The celibate (single) person dedicated their life to prayer, service to the poor, and living in community as those who, because they were joined to the church, were married to Christ.

Whatever meaning martyrdom had in those first few hundred years was poured into marriage and into monasticism, the primary place for celibate life. The Eastern Church crowned husband and wife with martyrs' crowns on their wedding day. And the ascetic life in a monastic community became an alternative (and prophetic) way of giving one's life away, learning how to love, and learning how to die. Marriage and celibacy were both filled with spiritual significance. There were cultural containers to hold both these paths of constraint.

Singleness

I have been using the term *celibacy*, which is more descriptive than our modern-day concept of singleness. Nearly a quarter of the adult population in America is single, but being single, even as a follower of Jesus, does not necessarily mean that one is thinking about singleness as a way that God is inviting them into ascetic constraint. There are many people considering what it means to live faithfully in their sexuality as followers of Jesus while also trying to become free of the purity culture that many of us—at least in my GenX/Xennial generation—were raised in. It's hard to cast a vision for the formational work of celibacy in a moment when many of my own peers are working through an array of complex trauma tied to their early sexual desires. This trauma is due in part to the heaps of shame prevalent in the evangelical subculture of the 1990s.

I've been in the middle of raising four girls. Conversations about sex and the goodness of sex and the greater good of sex within marriage are delicate, but we're having them with, I hope, some healthier ways of thinking than purity culture and the shame it has wrought.

The critique of the purity movement is centered on the reality that both the consequences of becoming sexually active and benefits of sexual purity were oversold. Purity culture idolized sexual "wholeness" in marriage and handed too much responsibility to girls for the lust of boys.[2] We were promised that physical and emotional safety were the sole privilege of those who waited to have sexual intimacy until marriage. And then many people got married having kept that pledge of purity only to realize that sex and sexual intimacy and the emotional wake of sex, even within marriage, is quite complicated. It turns out that the passions we've been talking about cannot be remedied by purity. Only love can heal the passions.

I believe that the nonmarried life is meant to be a celibate life because sex is meant to be practiced within marriage. This still seems to be the consensus of global Christianity. But I wonder if we can go one step further? Wesley Hill quotes his friend Eve Tushnet, who said, "You cannot have a vocation to '*No.*'" Both Wes and Eve speak about celibacy within the LGBTQ+ conversation. Hill goes on to say,

> You can't build your life around something that you are saying 'no' to. You have to embrace a sense of purpose and calling. You are being ushered into a life of discipleship into God's kingdom. And any account that we offer of the transformation of sexual desire in celibacy . . . has to not simply leave people with a command to refrain from something; it has to beckon us into a life of hospitality and community and friendship and discipleship in which celibates can find [their] desires transformed.[3]

Within the church we need a positive vision for singleness as celibacy in order to infuse the single life once again with the intentional formational possibilities it had when the church held celibates in a meaningful *way of life*. The path of monasticism and religious orders is not the only way to do this, although, of course, this is a possible way for some.[4]

The Constraint of Love

On the surface, marriage and celibacy appear to be radically different ways of life. But they share something in common. They each provide a constraint on our desires and longings, which results in a more focused, refined, and powerful form of love.

Imagine with me for a moment how water flows out the end of a hose. Without a nozzle that is able to adjust the flow of water, the water just spills out without a tremendous amount of force. But if you want to wash your car or clean up a mess, you want the water to come out in a more concentrated form. A nozzle *narrows* the opening of the hose so the water comes out with greater force. The constraint at the end of the hose focuses the flow of water more potently. Marriage and celibacy both work in this way. The constraints that each of these vocations provides refine and focus our love. Our love is given more force when the desires that drive it are narrowed and directed by the many deaths contained in each of these ways of life. Ultimately, this narrowing of our loves points us toward and helps us become present to the divine love that God has placed inside of us.

We learn to love with the love that God pours out into our hearts. This comes, as the apostle Paul has articulated, through the sufferings that the constraint provides. And the suffering produces perseverance, which produces character and ultimately hope. These are the conditions through which we become most present to the love of God being poured out into our hearts (Rom 5:3-5).

Marriage and celibacy are both vocations that constrain our love. There is a way of thinking about marriage or celibacy as a calling to embrace. Both forms of life offer a constraint of a particular kind of desire, a kind of love, that we often only connect with sexuality but actually has a deeper foundation than merely the desire for sex. This kind of desire is what philosophers and theologians have called *eros*. We have a hard time imagining *eros* apart from our understanding of *eroticism*, but sexual desire is only part of how we ought to think about *eros*.

Eros is like a furnace of desire glowing red hot inside of us. Perhaps this is even the furnace that boils the water that produces the steam in that little room where the passions get released with either a slow-release valve or a quick-release valve. Eros more or less is the desire that drives us to exert our self into the world and attempt to take it in. It shows up quite naturally in our physical body as a sexual drive.

But this furnace of desire is primarily one that burns with both the desire to be loved and the desire to love. (It also burns with a desire for beauty.) We feel the heat of this furnace in some of life's most beautiful moments—the birth of a child, the final movement of a symphony, or sexual intimacy encountered in self-giving love. And it is the heat of this fire that we feel even in religious experiences in prayer or worship or service among the poor. Ronald Rolheiser says that it's a fire that has been placed there by God: "Inside us there's a divine fire, a greatness, that gives us infinite depth, insatiable desire, and enough luminosity to bewilder every psychologist."[5] In these beautiful moments, where we are nearly overwhelmed with desire, we tap into the divine love that is continually being poured out into us and into the world.

We also can feel this fire flare up in painful moments. It pulsates when the love we want does not come to us—moments when we are rejected or when we feel the lack of affection from someone that we're seeking it from. These moments become like bellows blowing onto fire with a longing for what we have not attained.

The desire to love and the desire to be loved is at the center of all our passions.

Before those passions are healed by the love of God, they present themselves as a lack of freedom. There are some things we feel like we must do and there are some things we really want to be able to do, but we can't seem to channel our energy in the right way. We try to satisfy the desire in ways that make us slaves to the desire. We look for love and give love away with short-sightedness (like Augustine). In short, we forget what the desire and the love is *for*. Or, as C. S. Lewis put it, "It would seem that Our Lord finds our desires not too strong, but too weak. We are half-hearted creatures, fooling about with drink and sex and ambition when infinite joy is offered us, like an ignorant child who wants to go on making mud pies in a slum because he cannot imagine what is meant by the offer of a holiday at the sea. We are far too easily pleased."

There has been much confusion about the spiritual disciplines and the tradition of asceticism. And much of this confusion has come from thinking that our spiritual training is somehow meant to reduce our desires. Sometimes it feels like we have too much desire—and this is what, so it seems, leads us to eat too much, and drink too much, and search for naked bodies on the internet. But really our desires are simply spilling out in the direction of things that don't satisfy us. Our desires are not focused in the right ways— and this has everything to do with inherited patterns of behavior from our families of origin and coping mechanisms and our efforts to soothe our trauma. Being human is really hard.

The ascetic tradition, and the whole tradition of practicing spiritual disciplines in community, is not really about reducing our desires but about diverting or modifying the way our desires are expressed. The practices of constraint are about *redirecting* our desires. We form rhythms of solitude and silence, for example, to direct our love for God toward God and to receive God's love. We worship and study and work with our bodies as ways of channeling that desire toward the love of God and learning how to receive God's love, which we believe, by faith, will help us also learn how to love our neighbor. But we are not trying to extinguish the fire (this was the method of the Puritans); we are trying to focus it on loving and receiving love. This is the method of the religious orders and the monastic streams. This giving and receiving love is what we were actually created for, being in the image of God and made to be like him. After all, God *is* love. Spiritual formation is our partnership with God to direct the power of that infinite fire toward God and God's purposes in the world.

God is the one who lit the fire. He is the one who gave us desire because we were created with the primary task of giving and receiving love. The furnace is God's furnace.

Consider another image offered by Gregory of Nyssa. Gregory's work influenced much of how the early church thought about desire and love, particularly in the way it was worked out in both marriage and celibacy. He was one of the Eastern Cappadocian fathers who contributed to our understanding of the Trinity through their work on the Nicene Creed. His writings influenced his brother Basil's own rule of life for the monastic communities he founded. His fingerprints are all over the tradition of monastic spirituality.

Gregory asks us to imagine a stream that flows from a spring. As this stream goes along it is divided quite randomly into a number of different channels or smaller streams. Eventually, the water just dissipates, and the force of the current becomes small because the water is going everywhere and nowhere in particular. The current that once carried large logs way upstream can now barely move a leaf along. Then he asks us to imagine being able to channel all of this dispersed water back into one stream—to bring the water into one particular place—like in an irrigation setup where water is moved from a river to a field in order to grow crops.

Unless our love is channeled, it dissipates.

Many Christians have historically understood marriage and celibacy as environments or "containers" where our desire and love can be directed so that the force of the current does not dissipate but gets stronger. The Christian answer to the question, "What do we do with all this burning desire to make my mark in the world?" is to get in touch with that desire so that it might be first *intensified* and then released to the praise and glory of God. Eventually, we discover that the stream of our love is being channeled toward God. We discover God's own love is being channeled toward us. And we, from this experience, learn how to love for the simple fact that he has first loved us. We get filled up with the love of God, and as we grow in our ability to steward the strength of desire, our love and desire are intensified by grace and we become participants of the divine love that has already been poured into our hearts.

This is God's plan for rescuing the world.

The Constraint in Marriage

Our love and desires are intensified and channeled within marriage in this way: We commit to learning how to love this one person in a unique way. We are allowed to love this one person in a way that no one else is allowed to love them. And they have committed to loving us in a way that no one else will have access to. We even get to practice this love with our bodies in a sexual relationship, though we learn quickly that as wonderful as this is, and as pleasurable as it can be, it alone cannot be the goal of our love, nor will it be able to sustain the contours of love. Sex is a wonderful way to love, but even this way of loving feels incomplete. Perhaps having a few kids under the age of ten running around helps us realize that there are now infinite (less exciting but nonetheless fulfilling) ways of loving our spouse. Even if no kids arrive, there is enough work and activity in the world to help us see our love and learn other forms of expression.

Two people in a Christian marriage vow to love one another in a way that puts on display Christ's love for the church—self-giving, self-sacrificing, self-forgetting. This is the slow process of learning how to give up one's life for the sake of the other. There are many deaths along the way and the only way that love comes from death is through tapping into the grace of God in prayer. And so we also learn how to pray.

We spend our life channeling much of our love toward this one person. This person receives our love in a singularly channeled way. And we learn that even when our love feels right—when there is patience and kindness and gentleness and even passionate lovemaking and all the other things we hope our love will contain— it is still not able to fill the infinite cavern that God has placed within the one we love. Only God can fill it. Maybe this takes a decade or more to truly understand.

We also learn that we cannot receive all of our spouse's love. And we learn that even if we could, it would not completely fill up the reservoir inside of us designed to be filled by love. Only God can fill it until it is full. This is what every saint has learned: there is an infinite place within us that can be filled only by God's own self.

In the end, what we learn in marriage is that given the permission to pour as much love into another as we know how, our love—our desire to love and be loved—is never quite fulfilled. The fire that lives inside of us is unable to be extinguished. And it does not run out. And, as exhilarating as this union of marriage is, it is a sign and symbol for a more infinite union with God. And so we turn our desire and love toward this more infinite possibility, toward God, which also causes our capacity to love within our earthly union of marriage to expand.

Our love and desire become intensified through our marriage.

The Constraint in Celibacy

Love and desires are also intensified and channeled within celibacy. Christopher Hall writes, "The church fathers generally view celibacy as a calling that directly and purposely challenges the normal rhythms and patterns of human life, a vocation possible only by the supernatural empowering given by God's grace."[6] Celibacy teaches us how to receive in a direct way, not mediated by another person, the strength of love and nearly infinite capacity to receive love. Celibacy is also a life that chooses to set aside the possibility of pouring one's fire of love, in all its fullness, into one other person. At first, the stream of love and desire feels as though it is blocked by a dam. *Where can all of this love be poured into?*

But slowly, the work of learning more about that desire over time begins to train the heart toward noticing the strength of desire and the longing to give oneself away. The celibate person also learns of their longing to receive another's fierce and full love. And the ache of not being able to do so is a kind of death.

The celibate knows the depth of the space within them ready to receive love. They also know that they have so much love to pour out—but where should this love be directed? A celibate feels this tension in their body most acutely through sexual desire. And this desire for sexual union becomes a lens through which the man or woman learns that their desire to be joined to another eventually leads them to a desire to be joined to God. And without sexual expression to release the strength of this fire, the celibate learns, perhaps more than those who are married, to offer their body as a living sacrifice, which is pleasing to God (Rom 12:1). Perhaps in a more direct way than in a marriage, a celibate learns to receive the love of God because God pours his love into their hearts through the Holy Spirit (Rom 5:5).

Over time, the celibate slowly learns, through growing attentiveness, to generously measure out their love to those in the community. They discover that they are not simply called to a "mandate of self-denial"[7] but to a life of learning how to dole out the fire, through the guiding of the Holy Spirit, in service of others. The death and surrender of loving erotically through one's body in sexual relationship gets resurrected into a life with a unique vocation of reimagining that *eros* toward the many.

Practicing Marriage

In the spring of 2022, *New York Times* opinion columnist Tish Harrison Warren wrote an excellent reflection on her marriage, admitting rather vulnerably that she "married the wrong person."[8] Twitter traffic threw her under the bus, citing the wonderful benefits of divorce, but Tish was not the first person to make such a claim. Theologian and ethicist Stanley Hauerwas came to an even broader conclusion. He says that all of us marry the wrong person:

> Destructive to marriage is the self-fulfillment ethic that assumes marriage and the family are primarily institutions of personal fulfillment, necessary for us to become "whole" and happy. The assumption is that there is someone just right for us to marry and that if we look closely enough we will find the right person. This moral assumption overlooks a crucial aspect to marriage. It fails to appreciate the fact that we always marry the wrong person.
>
> We never know whom we marry; we just think we do. Or even if we first marry the right person, just give it a while and he or she will change. For marriage, being [the enormous thing it is] means we are not the same person after we have entered it. The primary challenge of marriage is learning how to love and care for the stranger to whom you find yourself married.[9]

The force of such a statement about "marrying the wrong person" quickly sums up what many of us have experienced in marriage: Learning to love (and die) in marriage is hard. And the results can be beautiful.

Learning to love in marriage is hard because there are so many things that need to die in us in order for our marriage to actually work. This dying process is also the process of our love being channeled. It's natural for our desire and energy to be dissipated in a thousand different directions. As our love is constrained and channeled into the marriage, we say goodbye to other pathways our love may have been expressed. We are limited and we cannot love in all directions. But what gets resurrected, because our desire and love has been intensified, is a love molded around the form proclaimed by the apostle Paul—a love that in some mysterious and sacramental way reveals the self-sacrificial love of God's own self.

One of the ways this death and resurrection cycle plays out is through discovering how our interior life is projected onto our marriage. The unhealed passions are slowly released throughout our marriage. Purity culture taught that getting married would somehow cure us of lust. And then we discover lust right there in the middle of marriage. We learn that sexual intimacy is actually more complicated than we thought it would be. Marriage reveals how the passions are at work within sexual intimacy, and even more so through the seasons where sexual intimacy is less available to us, either physically or emotionally.

We go through seasons where we fight against some version of acedia (boredom) simply trying to figure out who has paid what bill, and who will be cooking dinner, and why the raccoons keep getting into the trash, and if we should homeschool the kids. We discover together that most of married life is very ordinary. And much of ordinary life does not live up to the idealized versions of married life that we had projected onto it since before we were married.

We settle into long stretches of sleepless nights when (if) the children arrive. There are months (and years) when we look to our spouse to give us more than they are designed to give us. The reality of the limitations of this relationship slowly settles in, and we discover envy inside of us as we look at the seemingly happy marriage of a coworker or a friend or a romance within the make-believe world of television. Or we escape into an imaginary version of our own marriage. *If only this could be different.*

We are quite certain that we are not the one in the wrong in this ongoing argument that we keep revisiting. In our pride we are unable to see the other's perspective. Until we finally do see it. And we realize that we were wrong all along, but it has taken years to come to this conclusion. It's been so long, in fact, that once we come to this conclusion the other person isn't even mad about it—but there is a twinkle in their eye when you are finally able to say that you are sorry. They reach in for a hug because they know the same is true of them.

And then there are those moments when those unhealed passions get released all at once—anger spills out, we say things we never intended to say out loud and now we can't take them back. We storm out the door and curse under our breath. Sometimes our curse is loud enough for the other to hear. We learn how to ask for forgiveness, and we learn how to forgive well beyond what we thought we had the capacity for. This is a small illustration of what it means to "marry the wrong person." It's just another way of saying what we've already discovered: we marry someone who is not *free*. And then we have the uncomfortable experience of realizing that the person we have married has also married someone who is not *free*. And now not only are we not entirely free from all that is not well in us, but we are also daily confronted with all that is not well in the other.

But slowly we also learn that we have a capacity to love and cherish far beyond what we thought we could. Our love has somehow become intensified. We taste the depths of joy and comfort beyond what we have ever been able to receive. Something very beautiful emerges from something that is very hard. I love the way Gregory of Nazianzus captures it: "Through marriage we become one another's hands, ears, and feet. Marriage doubles what had been weak . . . sorrows shared hurt less; joys shared are sweeter for both."[10]

One invitation, among many, within this vocation of marriage is to *practice* allowing the "container" of marriage to be the place where we become more deeply aware of how we are not able to act in the freedom of loving this person in the way we wish we could, and how they are not able to love us in the way we want to be loved. At least in the beginning. We find ourselves again staring at the inevitability of our weakness, crying out for the help of God. Marriage is an easy place to become present to this and, in doing so, to nurture humility. Which means that marriage becomes a place where we are also able to discover the way the love of God is mediated through another person to nurture the healing that God is doing in us.

All of this takes a tremendous amount of *practice*—years of practice—in order for it to unfold.

My experience of marriage to Jaime has felt, at times, like I "married the wrong person." But I've discovered that this person has grown to love me more than anyone else in the world. And that I have learned to love her more than I have ever been able to love anyone. There is no doubt that iron sharpens iron. And we have slowly changed into people who love more deeply than we previously were able to.

We discover over and over again that we are stuck in some pattern that requires one or both of us to change. There simply is no way around this. When we're in these seasons of being stuck, we discover that each of us brings a part of us that is on autopilot.

Our habits of marriage are ingrained in a way that we can't seem to break free from. It's like we can't *not* fall into that broken pattern. The same argument plays out in a predictable way. We both respond in ways that are unhelpful. And then we later realize what might have been more helpful, or more loving, or more trusting. What we need in those moments is transformation of our marriage *habitus.* Our *way of life* with one another needs the freedom that only self-surrender can lead us toward. We close our eyes and cry out to God for help. And eventually our hearts are softened to one another. I'm not a hundred percent sure how it happens, but for us at least, we have incrementally discovered layers of healing, deepening of forgiveness, and opportunities for self-sacrifice. We have been changed by this mysterious process.

It has felt like death and resurrection.

In marriage, we either embrace with humility the reality that we have a high capacity to hurt another person—and that we are causing hurt for this one who we are meant to love as Christ loves the church—or we remain inattentive to this reality. But our inattentiveness means that we move through life without being willing for the other's needs and desires to create real and permanent change in us. At stake in all of this is our own identity. *This is just who I am! How can I be me when being me causes so much pain for the person I pledged my life to?*

In some very real sense, it is impossible to remain who you are while also learning how to love in the way that God loves. If I remain as I am, I cannot learn the love of God. The love of God will change me. Learning requires change.

The biggest struggle in a marriage is not allowing oneself to be changed by it.

If I view my marriage as a place of formation, I can learn and grow in a way that will inevitably invite me to make serious changes to who I am—or at least who I imagine myself to be. In marriage we learn to exchange these superficial things that I'm attached to about myself or my personality for God-birthed things. I will become more fully *who I am*. The truest version of who God has made me is a person who is able to love with self-sacrificial love. Marriage is one of the tutors helping me learn to be who God already determined that I would become when he made me according to his image and gave me his Spirit to transform me into his likeness.

In marriage we also embrace, again with humility, that we have a high capacity to love another person and that they also have a high capacity to love us. We make decisions to help this other person pursue their lifelong dream. We take on debt. We move to a new city. We slow our life down and find that the thrill of giving this one person the deepest part of our love is far more exhilarating than the ambitious thing we had hoped to accomplish five years ago but would have required us to be less attentive to dying for the sake of this other person.

Marriage as a *practice*—as a lifelong discipline of training—is allowing the love of God to come through this other person to me in order to teach me about love. It is also allowing this person's life to reflect back to me the insufficiency of my love for them and of their love to me. And this reminds us both of the sufficiency of God's love. It is also the practice of understanding that whatever depth of love I want to give or whatever depth of love I desire to receive is not fully satisfied through this other person. But this marriage, my marriage, has become something through which the love of God can come.

Practicing Celibacy

Very few people in our culture have been invited into the intentional work of formation in the celibate life. Few have been given any opportunity to discern a potential vocation, a sense of calling, to live in a celibate life. The single/celibate life is often viewed, particularly in our default-to-marriage Christian subculture, as a holding pattern *until* marriage. The idea of singleness as a semi-permanent or permanent calling—one discerned in community through prayer—has mostly been relegated to priests. I had never even heard celibacy addressed as a topic of conversation in a non-Catholic context until just a few years ago. And yet in the first five hundred-plus years of the church, celibacy was by far considered the *preferable* calling.

Over the last decade, it has been those navigating same-sex attraction within the church who have begun to talk about being *called* to celibacy. Numerous men and women have taken up the language of celibacy and resurrected it as a vocation, a calling, within the church's ongoing discernment on issues of sexuality—particularly for those who experience same-sex attraction.[11] This perspective helps the conversation move beyond questions that try to force us into the overly simplistic categories of *affirming* or *nonaffirming*.

Before we go too far down the path of imagining celibate vocations making their way back into the church, it's important to note some places of resistance. Many of my gay or lesbian Christian friends have expressed that when their nonaffirming churches declare celibacy as their only option, it feels like something being forced on them. I do not believe celibacy should be forced on anyone or required of anyone in order for that person to stay connected to and be a vital part of a community.[12]

Other gay friends have expressed that their affirming friends and institutions do not understand or support the choice to pursue a life of celibacy. Many who are affirming feel suspicious of the celibacy conversation. Twitter threads have blown up with assumptions and accusations when someone who is gay considers celibacy as a lifelong vocation because this is the invitation they have felt through their reading of the Scriptures. It's as though one person choosing a path of constraint is an act of aggression toward those who have not come to the same conclusion. This makes sense given how violent and abusive the church has been toward our gay and queer brothers and sisters.

For me, as a married man with four children, this topic feels vulnerable to talk and write about. If I may, I'd like to speak directly to gay, lesbian, and queer readers. As a pastor my heart is on fire with a pastoral love for those with same-sex attraction trying to understand God's invitation to them. I believe that you should have full agency in determining whether you are called to lifelong celibacy. My hope is that you are surrounded by a Christian community that does not overdetermine the outcome of this decision for you. A vocation of celibacy should be discerned over a long period of time within Christian community. This could and should be happening for *both* gay and straight men and women in our churches. Celibate vocations should not *only* be occupied by those who are same-sex attracted. This lifelong vocation should be more broadly considered in local church life.

This is not meant to be a chapter that dives deep into the ongoing discernment and deliberation regarding same-sex sexuality.[13] But to talk about celibacy in this present cultural moment requires us to be honest about the shape of the conversation. And at the center of this conversation right now are gay and queer men and women who are wondering if Jesus is calling them toward a life of celibacy. And if this is so, my hope is that we might consider how this *calling* might be celebrated. It seems these men and women are the only ones talking about vocational celibacy. I think we need to learn from how this conversation is unfolding.

The modern Western church has failed to nurture the celibate vocation. We have neglected, more generally, to teach and lead people toward even imagining that this way of life is *possible*. We have overemphasized marriage and family life in a way that has left behind one of the primary prophetic modes of living within the early church. At the same time, Christian marriage has failed at almost exactly the same rate as non-Christian marriage. To now attempt to retrieve celibacy as a sacred calling—while only imagining that it would be filled by gay or queer celibates—lacks integrity. As a whole, the Western church has lost the vision for celibate vocations. We are, so to speak, out of practice.

To expect gay and queer brothers and sisters to alone bear the burden of revitalizing celibate vocations is too much to ask. If celibacy is even to be an option for some people regardless of sexual orientation or attraction, the church will need at least a generation to reimagine the future of celibate vocations. Nearly all the support structure and social imagination within our churches is for marriages and families. If we are going to become a church that practices celibate vocations once again, it will require recovering an infrastructure that the church once had but has nearly abandoned. The infrastructure that can hold celibate vocations is one in which people practice a set of shared common commitments together not only for their own sake but for the sake of one another. The primary institution that has held the celibate vocation is that of religious orders. This is part of why I think we need to reimagine what these religious orders might become in the twenty-first century.

My hope is that we can also begin cultivating the gift of celibacy even for those who do not sense a call to the new forms of religious vocation that might emerge from the resurgence of interest in religious orders, rule of life, and taking vows. The gift and graces of vocational celibacy have in many ways been *hidden* within the priesthood and traditional vocations within the Catholic church. And yet every person begins their adult journey in a state where they could "try on" the celibate life. We might consider reimagining "singles ministry" around long-term discernment of whether God is presently calling someone to pursue the vocation of marriage or the vocation of celibacy. This could decenter sexual intimacy in the conversation about celibacy. The practice of celibacy is not centered around what one does with one's genitals. The historic framework of celibacy has always been about love and desire and the infinite longing that God has placed in the human being. A call to lifelong celibacy is a true and prophetic vocation as a means to participation with God in directing those desires back to God and into the world through becoming an instrument of God's love for others.

I have a friend, Heather, one of our own vowed members in the Order of the Common Life, who has discerned a call to vocational celibacy. As she has gone deeper into this work of allowing her desire and love to become channeled through the constraints of her celibate life, she has discovered that it has led her not to less love within human relationships but to more. Heather says: "My celibate vocation is not a free pass from the refining work of deep committed relationships. I just have to be intentional about choosing to continue to put myself into relationships within community that give me opportunity to learn how to love and be loved. I have had to learn how to cultivate these kinds of relationships in ways that are very similar to the married people I know who are learning how to cultivate loving and being loved within their marriage."[14]

Celibacy is not practiced alone. We might even consider dropping the vocabulary of *singleness*. As Karen Keen writes,

> "Singleness" as we conceive of it in our culture is not the will of God at all. It is representative of a deeply fragmented society. Singleness in America typically means a lack of kinship connectedness. This was not the case, for example, with Jesus who was not married. He never lived alone. He went from the family home to a group of twelve close friends who shared daily life with him until he died (followers who would have never left off following him). His mother and brothers were also still involved in his life and are often mentioned. Jesus' mother was there at his darkest hour when he died. In contrast, singleness in America often refers to a person who lives alone or in non-permanent, non-kinship relationships.[15]

In order to welcome the practice of celibacy we will need to create pathways within our local churches and emerging religious orders for people to discern the shape of celibate life that deeply integrates into the lives of others.

The Freedom to Love

When our love and desire are constrained and channeled, what we finally come to gain is, ironically, a more intensified love. We gain the freedom to love because our unhealed passions of lust and pride and envy and all the rest are squeezed out and brought to the surface. This happens both in the weight and joy of marriage and in the ongoing learning environment of celibacy across relationships within the community. In the end, we learn the love of God and how to love as God loves. We learn "the patience to bear the tension of the interminable slowness"[16] of the whole process.

Ronald Rolheiser calls this patience, this process of waiting for these environments to do their work, *chastity*. Chastity has traditionally been understood to relate to only the sexual side of *eros*. But Rolheiser expands the idea to include all the other ways that that furnace of desire and love learn to deal with the passions. To be chaste, as Rolheiser is reimagining it, is to be patient with the tension of not quite consummating our loves in the exact way we wish we could. And this happens both in marriage and in celibacy.

We slowly learn, in either container, that when we love and are loved by another human, we also grow in our love for God. Receiving love from another allows us to grow in our receptivity to the love of God. The opposite is also true. As we grow in our capacity for the love of God, we grow in capacity to love others.

Sixth-century monk Dorotheus of Gaza gives us an image of a circle where we and those we hope to grow in love for are standing along the circumference of a circle. God is in the center.

> Let us suppose that this circle is the world and that God himself is the center: the string lines drawn from the circumference to the center are the lives of human beings. . . . Let us assume for the sake of the analogy that to move towards God, then, human beings move from the circumference along the various radii of the circle to the center. But at the same time, the closer they are to God, the closer they become

to one another; and the closer they are to one another, the closer they become to God.[17]

In marriage, our love becomes intensified in our pursuit of loving another—and this leads us toward a greater discovery of God's love and a greater capacity to love God. Movement toward our spouse ultimately also leads us toward God. In celibacy, our love is intensified in God and God's love is intensified in us, which leads us to move toward others with a desire to love. Movement toward God leads a celibate person toward others because God is on mission to the whole world with his love. Getting close to the heart of God leads to love of others.

Certainly the way this works out in real life is not as clean as lines in a circle—but in both celibacy and marriage our love is being perfected and completed and refined in both directions—toward God and toward others. With married people and celibates living in community together, ideally, the church then becomes a beautiful representation of the fulfillment of the two greatest commandments—to love God and to love others.

PRACTICING
MARRIAGE AND CELIBACY

For Pastors and Leaders

If you are a pastor in the daily work of caring for people, you know that a lot of formational work happens in the context of marriage. Some larger churches have staff designated for marriage ministry. You might consider developing a vision in your church for helping singles discern whether they are called to marriage. The assumption within most families is that kids grow up and get married. I imagine that this will continue to be the cultural norm, though if we reimagine celibate vocations, we'll need to create structures within our local churches to support those in discernment of either marriage or celibacy. And, if celibacy is going to be a real option, some of the resources in our churches will need to be allocated not just to singles ministry but to ministry to those who are taking on a lifetime commitment to singleness as celibacy and as a calling to live prophetically in the world.

❖ Take a season to explore more about the conversation around celibacy from within the gay-Christian perspective. These men and women are stewarding a challenging conversation. The primary organizing group for this conversation is Revoice (revoice.us).

❖ Read Wesley Hill's book *Spiritual Friendship* with your staff team or leaders. Wes's book is a beautiful look at the formational capacities of navigating celibacy.

❖ When you preach about marriage, consider talking about it as a form of *asceticism*. We can serve marriages best by helping young people in particular understand that spiritual formation and following in the way of Jesus primarily teaches us how to give up our life for the sake of another. To do this well, we'll also need to teach and equip married couples to see how this narrative about giving up one's life can mask deep problems of codependency.

❖ Normalize therapy for folks in your local church.

For Small Groups

This conversation in a small group has the potential to bear wonderful fruit. Ideally, the room would include both married couples and singles. It's unlikely that someone who is single in your group has taken on a formal lifelong vow of celibacy. Most single people I know are still wanting to find a spouse. But I've also met a number of singles who are considering (discerning) singleness for life as a way of situating their life in a category historically held by the church (celibacy).

Give the group time to prepare for the discussion questions below. For example, assign a few people a specific date when they will share their own experience. This way, couples can prepare ahead of time and agree on what they are ready to share. The vulnerability of a couple in a group can help create deeper relationships. But if one person within a couple shares beyond what the other person in the relationship is ready to disclose—this could shut the couple (and the group) down.

Take a season for your group to lean into this conversation together. Take it slow and make a schedule for both singles and couples to have an opportunity to reflect and share. You might consider making your group "closed" for the season this topic is discussed.

Here are some discussion questions:

For Married Couples:

Share with the group about a time that your marriage has felt like a container that is teaching you about how to love more deeply. What are some of the big lessons of love in your marriage? What have been some of the hard things?

Share with the group a time that you learned how to receive love from your spouse in a way you hadn't before. How has God demonstrated his love for you through your spouse?

What has God asked you to lay aside for the sake of your marriage? What needs to die? Have you shared this with your spouse?

For Singles:

How did you react to this chapter on marriage and celibacy? What did it stir up for you?

How has your singleness been a container for you to learn the love of God? Have you had particular seasons when you've learned more about God's love through your singleness?

Share about a time that your singleness has been an opportunity to love more deeply.

Have you ever considered a lifelong call to singleness/celibacy? What does it feel like to even ask yourself this question?

For Parents

The best way to help your children to understand what marriage is for is to talk in age-appropriate ways about its joys and challenges. Include language about "learning how to love." When we make mistakes in our marriage in front of our kids, saying something as simple as, "I'm still learning how to love like God loves us!" will communicate how marriage is a relationship where our loves and desires are refined.

❖ Tell stories about your marriage to your kids. Normalize the refining seasons. *That was a really good season where we learned how to love one another. We really learned how to love each other when mommy took that new job.*

❖ If you are divorced and parenting alone, find ways to talk about your singleness or your previous marriage in ways that are both vulnerable and age appropriate.

❖ Invite single people into your home to share your table. Help your children understand that there are adults who live alone and do not have families. One of the ways that families can support single people, regardless of whether they have a lifelong commitment to singleness, is to help foster a sense of "extended family" for singles within your church community.

❖ As your kids grow older, rather than assuming that marriage is a certain outcome for them, take on a posture of curiosity. *Do you think you'll get married some day? Can you imagine yourself living single?* There is no need to encourage them toward either vocation—they'll sort that out. But understanding that there is more than one potential outcome could help pave the road for a process of discernment later on.

❖ As your children grow into teenagers, have frequent conversations about Western culture's oversexualization of our lives and bodies. You can have honest conversation with your teenage kids about sex while encouraging them to think about their own sexuality. There are ways to talk about sex and encourage kids to see sex as a beautiful way of expressing love within a lifelong partnership. But this conversation doesn't need to be driven by fear or use the old purity-culture tactics of scaring kids into thinking that if they become sexually active they are somehow blemished forever. There is a great deal of evidence that suggests otherwise. In the end, kids should recognize the power of sexual intimacy as that of giving and receiving love. Ideally this kind of intimacy is saved for marriage. But our kids and teens must know and feel at the depths of who they are that the most important part of the story of the Scriptures is the love of God.

❖ Tell your kids often about the love of God. For you and for them. I have laid a foundation for parents to ensure that their kids understand the fundamentals of God's love in my book *Imaginative Prayer: A Yearlong Guide to Your Child's Spiritual Formation* (IVP 2017).

Part Three

CONSTRAINTS
WE CONSENT TO

CHAPTER EIGHT

FORMATIONAL HEALING

CONSENTING TO THE CONSTRAINT OF ONE'S OWN STORY

The Freedom from Disordered Attachments

*"Where were you, Lord? Why did you not appear
at the beginning to end my pains?"*

*"I was here, Anthony," a voice answered, "but I waited to
see your struggle. Because you have remained firm and
have not yielded I will always be your helper."*

ATHANASIUS, *LIFE OF ANTHONY*

We do not yet know the value of the riches of Christ. This is why the apostle Paul calls these riches "unfathomable" (Eph 3:8). Paul's prayer for us—and our prayer for ourselves and one another—is that we might be able to comprehend what we are *not yet able* to comprehend. How do we come to know the love of Christ that surpasses our ability to know?

We often assume and we are culturally conditioned to believe that we grow through winning victories and overcoming challenges. We often live as though our knowledge of God's love and our apprehension of the unfathomable riches of Christ comes through perfecting our spiritual craft in some way.

But it is most often, if not always, quite the opposite.

My greatest hesitation in writing a book on practices of constraint (as a way of reframing the spiritual disciplines) is the possibility that you, dear reader, would come to this work through the well-worn path of *perfecting* the spiritual practices. The last thing I want you to feel is some version of *I need to try harder.*

The temptation we face when we finally become attuned to the need to lean into our spiritual formation is almost always that of striving. The invitation from God is, I think, a little different. The invitation is toward a radical consent to the reality of our life and honesty about our stories and the places in us in need of love and healing. This is how we begin to fathom the unfathomable riches of Christ. We let all the parts of us become open to the healing work of God.

The practice of formational healing is allowing God access to every part of your life that God wants to be present to in a particular way in this moment, and then joining God there.

But this process isn't passive. The practice of joining God in our healing leads to our freedom. In no way is our posture in the spiritual journey entirely passive. Some of the early contemplative communities, resting on an even earlier faulty theology, went so far in their total reliance on the grace of God that they failed to be active participants in the work of God. Paul reminds Timothy that the life of following Jesus should model a hardworking farmer, a soldier in preparation, and an athlete in training.

There is hard work.

And there is preparation.

And there is training. But training is not meant to help us *feel* stronger. We train in order *to see* the depth of our need and reliance on God. Constraint nurtures the power of God in our weakness. The spiritual life, at least within the tradition of the contemplatives, bends us toward humility.

We grow in freedom to the extent that we grow in awareness of God's love. And this awareness is revealed more in places of darkness where God shines a light than in any other place in our life. We experience the love of God and the unfathomable riches of Christ in the deepest ways when we can finally see, without shame or condemnation, the deepest wounds that sin has inflicted on us, when we can see how we have participated in those wounds and see also how God tends to them with the love of a Father. The process of formational healing frees us of the things we are attached to in ways that are not congruent with the work of God in our lives.

Athanasius tells the story of Anthony, one of the first desert fathers to go out into the wilderness and live in a cave. Athanasius's account is not a biography in the way we would understand this term, though most scholars agree that much of what Athanasius writes is true to some degree. But the story is also purposely embellished to paint the picture of Anthony's life in a way that inspires others to a life of solitude and asceticism.

One of the things that comes through quite clearly is that Anthony did a great battle against the demons who taunted him and lashed out against him. The stories of Anthony fighting off the demons in prayer, wrestling and struggling through the night, and standing up with great boldness with only the help of God can serve as a metaphor for the ongoing work of what I call "formational healing." Anthony struggled against these forces of darkness for much of his life. He spent years battling unwanted thoughts and afflictions. This will also be true of us. But Anthony engaged in much of his struggle alone. This should *not* be true of us. In order for true change and freedom to come to us, it will include others in the process.

Anthony's ongoing battle is the part of the story that most intrigues me. If Athanasius wanted a hero who was unaffected by struggle and untouched by anxiety, depression, and sleepless nights, he could have crafted one. But this would not have been a real hero because we would not be able to relate to him. Anthony's struggles against supernatural temptations gained so much popularity because in his struggle inside the darkness of a cave, we can see our own struggle. This is why he is said to be the father of early monasticism. He passed on, through his life, what so many of us experience when the comforts of our attachments are removed. We cry out to God alongside Anthony, "Where were you, Lord? Why did you not appear at the beginning to end my pains?" And with the psalmist David, "Hear my prayer, O Lord, and give ear to my cry; Do not be silent at my tears" (Ps 39:12). Anyone who has gone to therapy or received prayer for inner healing or continued to bump up against the same things over and over in conversation with a spiritual director knows well the prayer, *Where were you, Lord? Why did you not appear sooner?*

I am relieved to know that one of the early fathers of spiritual training struggled so vividly against spiritual and psychological forces.[1] But what is often overlooked in the praise of Anthony is a part of his approach that must be remedied in our own practices of constraint. For the most part, Anthony struggled all alone. He lived alone. He prayed alone. And he fought for his healing alone. Would his struggle have been lesser if he had gone through it alongside others?

The monastic model that Anthony gave us as a "solitary" eventually was replaced by a communal model with men and women sharing in a common rule of life. Works such as *The Sayings of the Desert Fathers*—a collection of sayings between teachers and students on their shared way of life—reveal how these men and women came together to learn from one another, support one another, visit one another, and care for one another. Anthony's struggle with "the beasts" in the wilderness was a necessary part of the tradition. And Anthony certainly had his visitors. But most of his struggle was alone.

I think nearly every one of us needs community in order to heal. In community we learn to tell one another the truest version of our story.

The Practice of Formational Healing

The healing of our soul can be a painful process. It is often slow.

God's healing power is his love, and he loves you and me uniquely within our own stories. God's love is universal and thus our healing is part of the healing of the cosmos—Christ came to save the cosmos (Jn 3:16; Col 1:20). Our story is part of a larger story of healing.

God's healing is universal. And God's healing is also unique to each one of us.

I call this unique work of God "formational healing." God is healing each and every bit of our unhealed passions (gluttony, lust, avarice, sadness, anger, acedia, vainglory, and pride) and all the wounds inflicted on us by other's unhealed passions. But he tends to each of us in unique ways.

Remember that image from John Cassian—the one where we are "thrown back" into God and rest on God with the assurance that God is *my* Father? Each one of us is meant to rest on God where God tends to each and every wound. The healing power is the love that God has poured out into us through the Holy Spirit and the simple fact that we are God's very own children.

Every one of us has a unique story with unique events that have shaped us.

My friend James recently shared with me some of his wife's story. When Tabitha was thirteen both her parents died in a car accident, immediately making her an orphan. For her entire high school experience she more or less parented herself. Imagine being parentless from age thirteen to thirty-eight (her present age). James went on to tell me that this part of her story isn't something that they've explored a lot in conversation. James wonders how this might be impacting Tabitha and their marriage. He wonders how it might impact their own parenting when their kids reach those high school years.

We are all shaped by the families we come from, the neighborhoods we are raised in, and the events that unfolded around us that were outside our control. Even as I write this, the stats on mental health are staggering as we emerge from a global pandemic. Teenagers especially are navigating dark times and will be unpacking these pandemic years well into their own adulthood. There is nothing that we can change about the global trauma we've all just experienced. It has forever shaped the future of everyone who lived through it. And, because of the ways we have changed these past few years, in all likelihood it will also shape future generations. We cannot change it, but we can heal from it. And we can heal from the ways that in our humanity we've come to rely on things in the world and patterns of thinking that bend us away from awareness of the love of God.

The practice of formational healing is the ongoing work of paying attention to the ways our life has, mostly without any conscious choice, bent toward self-preservation and self-protection and otherwise put our deepest needs "on the shelf" and left unattended. We have become attached to things and people and comforts, and we have grabbed on to particular outcomes to the problems we face. And many of these attachments bring a great deal of suffering to our inner world.

Any good trauma-informed therapist will tell us that our personality, our quirks, the ways we do conflict, and all our default ways of being are built on skills we developed along the way—primarily in the places of our first formation (family of origin)—to simply survive in the world we're living in. Our brains and bodies are really good at survival. And eventually some of what helped us survive in our younger years gets in the way of our present life. We have learned to avoid pain and seek out pleasure, which in many ways is good. But some of the pain we've sought to avoid is stuffed down so deep that it leaks out as we relate to others. And some of the pleasures we enjoy might be dulling us to the greater invitations of God—invitations to take risks or live generously or practice hospitality or relinquish our own way or love our enemies.

Those on the contemplative journey have often been accused of "navel gazing." And yet I've never met someone who is deepening their love and compassion for others who has not also already grown in compassion for their own self. But this growth in love and compassion for self is a long journey, often accompanied by real grieving work. We are very often unaware that the ways we have avoided pain and overly attached to pleasure stand in the way of these deeper invitations toward becoming who God is making us. Formational healing is the process of becoming more aware of this and saying *yes* to each invitation along the way.

The practice of formational healing attends to the questions: What is God's current invitation to me toward healing the different parts of my own story? What is God's current workmanship in the deepest places of my life? Who is walking next to me in these areas?

Consenting to the Constraints of Our Own Story

There are things about my life and about my story that have resulted in built-in constraints. Many of these built-in constraints are things I have chosen. I married fairly young. We had children young—four of them! I studied philosophy in college thinking I would get a PhD and become a professor. I didn't become a philosophy professor, which meant that I struggled to find a vocational path in my early- to midtwenties. I was constrained in ways I hadn't anticipated. My short foray into wearing a chef's coat was part of that struggle. There are countless ways in which both good and bad decisions constrained my life in both good and challenging ways. I suspect you could think of ways your own decisions have provided similar constraints. We buy houses. We take on student debt. We volunteer at a nonprofit. Nearly every choice we make brings with it built-in constraints on our time, our energy, and our financial resources. This is normal.

But there are also constraints on our lives that we have not chosen. There are circumstances around us that shape us in ways we never even had a hand in. Since 2016 we have lived in one of the historically poorest neighborhoods in our city. I've been exposed to new kinds of stories over the years of living here. I've tried to listen to the stories of my unhoused friends especially. Many of their lives shifted in tragic directions at a young age due to parental abuse or drug abuse or history of mental illness in the family. So much outside their control—and much of it before they even left home. I think about the different constraints that those first-formation stories have placed on my friend's lives.

You may, even now, be beginning to imagine the ways that your life has been constrained or limited by pieces of your story that you did not choose. Perhaps you have felt unexplainably tethered to some belief or deeply embedded pattern of thinking. These patterns of thinking may not presently result in unhealthy coping mechanisms—though you may not be able to see the whole impact of these patterns of thinking. At the very least, perhaps you can see pieces of this part of your story showing up as thin threads woven throughout multiple areas of your life. Barely noticeable but clearly out of place. This is also normal.

There are parts of my life and my story that I have had very little or no control over, and these too have provided some very real (and unwanted) constraints on my life. Some have been from my own family of origin. But other things have happened to me in my adult years that have left an impact on me—constrained me—in ways that I hadn't anticipated being constrained. Sometimes, the impact of these has been far greater than I first realized.

● ● ●

In January 2021, in the middle of the Covid-19 pandemic, my oldest daughter turned seventeen. This didn't feel eventful at the time. We have a lovely and close relationship. She was as ready for adulthood as any teenager I'd met. But as I sat down to write her birthday letter—something I do for each of my girls on their birthday—I felt a swell of emotion bubble up. Most of this was fairly normal, but there was something a little deeper that I was getting in touch with as I began to imagine her leaving home. I began to feel a nagging bit of anxiety about it. I prayed about it. I talked with my wife about it. I even mentioned to my daughter how emotional I felt about this milestone. It took me nearly three months to finish writing that birthday letter! It was a lovely father-daughter moment as she watched me navigate new territory. Hold on to this part of the story. I'll come back to it.

A few months later, my three oldest daughters were in a hit-and-run car accident. My oldest was driving and was clipped by a pickup truck while she was merging onto the highway. My 2007 Honda Element flipped over and bounced off a concrete wall before coming to a stop in the middle of the interstate. The truck that clipped them never stopped. Thankfully people pulled over and rushed to their aid. My fourteen-year-old remembers dangling upside down while people tried to get into the vehicle to help them out. Finally, a man busted one of the windows, cut the seatbelts and helped them crawl out to safety. My oldest daughter had called me while they were still upside down in the vehicle, relatively calm (most likely in shock) but clearly shaken.

This took place less than two miles from my home. After receiving the call from my daughter, I drove to their location, parked under the highway overpass, and full of adrenaline, scaled an overpass bridge where the accident took place in order to get to their location. When I arrived, they were huddled together, embracing one another, and crying. They were standing next to their flipped vehicle in the chilly early morning hours of an Ohio spring day. They seemed fine physically, but we rode to the hospital to get them checked out.

Over the next few weeks we slowly processed the accident. Every one of us had experienced trauma. We had a great support system checking in on us, caring for us, and helping our kids process what had happened. Over the next month, however, I noticed that every time my oldest daughter called me on the phone, my immediate thought was, "She's been in a car accident!" My heart rate would spike, and I would answer the phone expecting a tragedy. This is what is known as a *trigger*. My brain had locked into the stimulus of seeing my daughter's name pop up on my cell phone and had associated this with the car accident. This is a classic trauma response. My body was responding in the same way it had responded that morning when I heard my daughter's shaky voice calling from inside an overturned car on the interstate. My mind and body were stuck. And nearly every time my daughter called me, my body would release adrenaline, my mind would tell a story about what was happening, and I would be overcome with fear until I answered the phone and heard that everything was okay. All of this was outside my conscious control. This entire process put another layer on an already anxious season.

At the same time this was unfolding, I was trying to navigate pastoring a small church through the pandemic. I was grieving the loss of community and trying to help others grieve their losses. I was reading about churches in our stage (just four years into planting) that were closing down. We spent a great deal of time in our community talking about grief and loss. We tried to help one another be present to the losses in our kids' lives, the illness and deaths from Covid of people we knew, and the loneliness and isolation that so many in our community were feeling. I was processing my own grief, helping other churches and pastors process their grief (as a friend and spiritual director), and wondering if our church community was going to make it through.

I began to see a counselor to process some of my own grief. This was just another step in the ongoing formational healing journey. And while processing the grief that I was able to name, I began to get in touch with grief that I had not yet been able to name. I talked about the fear I felt in the wake of the car accident and my ongoing (irrational) fear that I was going to lose my kids in a tragic accident. My brain was stuck on this possibility as a result of the trauma of getting to the top of that bridge and seeing my oldest three girls standing next to a flipped vehicle while morning traffic was backed up for miles. I processed this event through a therapeutic modality called EMDR, which can help the brain process and release trauma in ways that talk therapy sometimes cannot. And through this process I gained access to other unprocessed grief and trauma going all the way back to some of my earliest memories. Grief and trauma are linked together like a chain. Once you start pulling, you often realize that there is more.

I processed the trauma of our second daughter's struggle with epilepsy in 2014, when over about eighteen months she had a seizure two to three times a week. I also gained access to previously untouched memories from my childhood. One was of my mother on the bathroom floor of the house I grew up in. She had nearly passed out from a miscarriage, and I discovered her there nearly unconscious. Somehow I managed to pick up the phone and dial a number for help. I checked in with my mom on this memory and learned for the first time that she had three miscarriages. She too remembers this moment. I was four or five years old.

Stored in my body and brain and memories was a younger version of myself who unknowingly and unconsciously decided— probably through an array of experiences but likely for the first time while I took on the role of rescuing my mother—that *he*, the little version of me, was responsible for taking care of people. This belief stuck to me. It co-opted my desire for something good—to love and care for others—and turned it into something less than good. Loving and caring for others is a natural impulse. But these good and natural impulses in us (desire and resistance) can easily become distorted. My desire to care for others was warped into a belief that I could and should *always* care for others. This became a belief that was deeply embedded in my story—all without any intention on my part.

This is an example from my own story of an unhealed passion. This is why, when I began to imagine my oldest daughter leaving college, a well of unnamable grief surfaced within me. *If she is gone, who will take care of her?* I can now name that emotion as sadness and my belief that I am the one that needs to take care of her as pride. But it wasn't a normal sadness. It was a sadness that had colored and was still coloring significant parts of my story. It wasn't a pride that was proud of anything in particular but a pride woven into the fabric of the way I saw the world.

Compare this good desire in me to care for others to the good desire for intimacy and connection in someone like Augustine, whose good desire was distorted into an insatiable one. This is why so much of his story centers around the unhealed passion of lust. But not just for sex. Augustine tells us in his *Confessions* that he wanted more of almost every pleasure. We don't just have one unhealed passion. All of them are unhealed to different degrees.

That is, until they are healed. And they *will* be healed. They will all be healed by the love of God.

The commitment to the practice of formational healing is to allow God to shine a light into the darkness of these interwoven and complex narratives of our own story. We begin the practice of formational healing when we can consent to the reality that the light of Christ is bright, and in the unexplored territory of our soul and story, there is still a great deal of darkness. And whatever that darkness is—trauma and wounds and oversized attachments—it is likely hindering our ability to say yes to all that God is inviting us into. Once we can consent to the reality that this is so, we can partner with God, in community, to join God in the work of our healing.

There is nothing to be ashamed of in this.

Who can free me from this? Thanks be to God.

It took nearly a year of prayer and spiritual direction and counseling and deepening friendship to stay present to this work of healing. I know that there is more of this work ahead. I've been untangling half a lifetime of beliefs and assumptions about the world and my role in it. I had already been aware of some of these patterns of belief through meeting with a spiritual director, but this season has brought a new level of healing.

But what exactly is being healed in this process?

The Freedom from Disordered Attachments

One of the most influential women in the earliest stream of the monastic tradition was Macrina the Younger. She created a community of women devoted to prayer and the study of Scripture,

living her life as a "mother" both to wealthy women who had re-
linquished their status and former slaves who sought out a life of
prayer. Macrina was the older sister of Basil the Great and Gregory
of Nyssa, both of whom became bishops and influenced the theological trajectory of the early church. Basil lived much of his adult
life in monastic communities of men practicing rhythms of prayer,
study, and work. While Gregory himself was not a monk (he was
married) it was nearly impossible to be a theologian in those years
without being influenced by the spiritual formation practices
pouring out of the monastic stream. Much of Gregory's influence
was in supporting his brother Basil's monastic program through
writing.[2] And it was the Rule of Basil and his work in integrating
this formational life into community that Benedict would later
read. It is hard to untangle the "influencers" in this tradition, but
no one would leave out Macrina, Gregory, and Basil as early
adopters and champions of the practical and theological traditions that produced the monastic movement and religious orders.

One of Gregory's most potent ideas, which continued to influence the monastic stream and the practice of asceticism, was
that the ultimate work of God is the purification of our soul
through his divine love. Gregory provides several images and
metaphors to get this point across, but the one I want to share
helps answer the question, why is this process so painful? In *On
the Soul and the Resurrection*, which is styled as a dialogue with
his sister Macrina while she is on her deathbed, there is a chapter
titled "Why Is Purification So Painful?" Here Gregory describes
being purified by God's divine love as a process similar to being
trapped under fallen debris after an earthquake.

Imagine the story of your life and all the unforeseen things
that have fallen to you. Or rather, on top of you. Life is like an

earthquake, isn't it? Now imagine that you and I are lying under rubble with wood and stone on top of us—these are the stories in our lives. Some of these stories impale us with protruding nails, piercing our skin and attaching themselves to us. Other stories we ourselves are holding on to, trying to grasp for anything sturdy or stable. We cling to things we think will protect us while we try to dig ourselves out and cry out for help.

Saint Ignatius of Loyola called these *disordered* (or inordinate) attachments.

Disordered attachments are things we become so attached to that they keep us from attentiveness to God. They push God out of the center of our lives and center on something else. These are some of the things that get in the way of our freedom.

Perhaps you've had a miscarriage and found yourself deep in a grief that will not go away. And in this grief you unconsciously cling to a story about love and loss, and this story plays like a soft soundtrack in the background. For some reason, you can't seem to get as close as you want to the people you love.

Or maybe you showed up with great vulnerability in a group of friends and that moment of exposure did not go as planned. So, probably without noticing it, you've armored up as a way of self-protecting. You haven't shared anything of real substance in years with anyone because some earlier version of yourself decided that nobody will ever understand.

Perhaps for as long as you can remember you have felt driven toward accomplishing and winning and being the one out in front of everyone else. You know the sting of watching someone else get the promotion and you notice that it's hard for you to celebrate with those who are "ahead" of you. There is a quiet voice inside of you whispering, *You have to climb to the top; that's the only place you'll ever be noticed.*

Or maybe you've never had the courage to speak with your real voice. You wonder if you have anything to say or if what you have to say would even matter. The inner voice says something like, *Better just to keep quiet, no need to rock the boat.*

Possibly you grew up in a family with an alcoholic and you never knew which version of that person was coming home. Would you be praised or criticized? *If you just do everything right and perfect nobody will be upset.* And so you've grabbed on to certainty and worn yourself out pursuing perfection.

The alcoholic mother; the miscarriage; the church that covered up a scandal; the spouse who cheated; your child's seizures in the middle of the night—this is the earthquake.

The self-protection and preservation; the conscious decision to keep quiet; the unconscious decision to wear yourself out with overwork; the need for things to be "just perfect" in order to feel calm; the belief that it is your job to take care of everyone—this is the rubble on top of us, some of which we've grabbed on to in order to feel safe.

Because of God's great love for us, says Gregory, he must pull us out of the rubble. He's rescuing us and restoring us as image bearers. His divine love is drawing us away from all that rubble and toward himself, and yet we tightly cling to all sorts of things, mostly unconsciously. That is, until we have the eyes to see it. But we only become aware of it when God, in his love, begins to pull us toward himself. This often happens when we are in a loving community committed to seeing both our wounds and the glory.

So God begins to pull on us, and then we have to consent to being pulled out. It's then that we notice that nails and splinters have pierced us and the heavy weight of the rubble is crushing our bones. And even when it is painful, God gently pulls while inviting us to let go—to stop clinging to the need to be great, or to be seen, or to be liked, or to be safe, or to be wealthy, or to have all the right answers. The invitation is to let go of the need to be in control or to avoid conflict at all costs because we grip so tightly to being at peace. God is in the process of *untying* us from all of this, and we are in the process of being *thrown back* into the love of God. God is clearing away the rubble to bring us to himself. Or as Gregory puts it, "The painful condition necessarily happens as an incidental consequence to the one who is drawn."

Gregory goes on to offer another image:

> Or if particularly sticky mud is plastered thickly around a rope, then the end of the rope is led through some small space, and someone pulls forcibly on the end of the rope towards the inside, necessarily the rope must follow the one who pulls, but the plastered mud must remain outside of the hole scraped off the rope by the forcible pulling. Because of the mud the rope does not move forward easily, but has to be pulled hard. Something like this I think we should imagine for the state of the soul. Wrapped up as it is in material and earthly attachments, it struggles and is stretched, as God draws his own to himself. What is alien to God has to be scraped off forcibly because it has somehow grown onto the soul. This is the cause of the sharp and unbearable pains which the soul must endure.[3]

To return to the metaphor from chapter four of the ways that we paint with counterfeit paints and muted colors over the image of God—which at our most basic level is who we are—we might imagine that God himself is doing the work of scraping off old paint from the canvas. He's working to restore the original image.

We might not like Gregory's image of God *forcefully* pulling upon us. We might not want God to start *scraping*. But the deeper I have gone into this work of formational healing, the more aware I become of the real power of sin (mine and others) that has done its work of corrupting very good things in me toward things that are not very good. The more I sit with men and women in spiritual direction, the more I see the soul-crushing quake of the world and the tenacity of God's love to rescue. If we can consent to the fact that both of these forces are at work in our lives, and if we can consent to the fire of God's love to purify us and burn up all that we are attached to that is not from God, then we will be free.

This is the same fire that sets us toward becoming *all flame*.

God begins this work when we die in baptism and join God's new-creation family, where others are doing that same work of allowing the love of God to burn up all that is not of God. But we have so often turned the family into a place where we present the best version of ourselves. We often don't make room for the wounds and the grief and the trauma to be welcomed in the church because the way those wounds and grief and trauma usually show up looks very much like sin. And so rather than consent to the truth of our own stories, we hide.

When we cling to material things (food, drink, sex, wealth, status) in order to cope—yes, we often are participating in *sin*. But the invitation toward a journey of formational healing is to not be too surprised or caught off guard by the presenting sin or disordered attachment. Focusing on the eradication of overeating, or porn addiction, or the hoarding of wealth might only manage the symptoms of a deeper problem. Trying to do this work alone is

counter to how the work of healing is supposed to work. Formational healing is the work of God's love to *heal* the particular form
of the disease that you and I carry, but this can only be done in
the presence of others because a great deal of God's love is mediated through the body of Christ. This love was first mediated
through signs and wonders from the hands of Jesus, then through
death and resurrection, and now through the body of Christ at
work in and through the church.

As the apostle Paul writes, "He who began a good work in *you*
will carry it on to completion" (Phil 1:6, emphasis added). It would
be better to translate it, "He who began a good work in y'all." The
"you" is plural. The work of God is nearly always mediated through
each other's words and love of one another. We'll explore how some
of this works in the practice of faults and affirmations (chap. 9) and
even more deeply through the practice of discernment in community (chap. 10).

I began this chapter with the idea that we do not yet know the
value of the riches of Christ. We are on a journey toward compre-
hending what is currently unfathomable. In the midst of our
painful process of healing, we also learn that very often the healing
is delayed. And sometimes it never fully comes.

If you've longed for inner healing, and for the pain to go away,
if you've prayed for it and cried out to God to meet you in that
deepest place of suffering, I see you. I'm naming the reality that
we often do not receive healing. But we do not learn the unfathomable riches of Christ *once we get healed*. We learn the riches of
God's love when we open ourselves up to the ongoing extrava-
gance of God's love *in the midst* of our ongoing suffering. We can
continue to long for and pray for healing, but one of the most
remarkable parts of the story we find ourselves in is that Christ is

the suffering one. He did not make any effort to avoid the suffering of the cross—and he will not avoid joining you again in the midst of your ongoing suffering.[4]

We do progress, though. We do the work of sitting in silence and asking God to speak to our hearts and reveal the areas of our lives that need his touch. This might come with just a gentle turn of our shoulders toward something very specific. I have watched a dear friend over the past six or so years become present to how little rest she gives herself. I've watched her bump up against the internal voice in her that says she must always be on the move and give till it hurts. I've watched her learn to practice sabbath, and I've been present in rooms where she has asked for others to reflect back to her what they see. She is dipping back into some therapy, coming back to some unhealed work she had begun previously. We've prayed with her and for her. And she just keeps receiving the love of God for her. In the end the love of God is enough. It may take her the rest of her life (and then some) to fully heal the passion of pride that drives her to try to rescue the world in a way that does damage to her own sense of self. I'm delighted to report that she is finding *rest*.

PRACTICING
FORMATIONAL HEALING

For Pastors and Leaders

Creating a culture of formational healing within our teams and churches begins, as all good leadership does, with ourselves. The first invitation in this work is for you to take an inventory of how you are personally doing in attending to your own inner healing. There are abundant resources for pastors and leaders to help us become present to the ongoing work of healing in our lives. God's primary work in the life of those oriented to the kingdom is a work of healing. Rather than rush to a specific resource for healing, consider first gathering people around you who are able to walk with you through whatever you might face as you begin or continue this work. Professional resources like therapists and spiritual directors are important, but more significant are *spiritual friendships.*

Spiritual friends are people who make sacrifices to know and love you—and you for them. Many pastors I meet are lonely and struggle to have the kind of friends that can care for them during periods of personal crisis. Pastors end up relying on boards and elders to be on the lookout for them—but friendship is different. Friendship isn't tied to a job or performance or "getting it right."

If you do not have these people in your life, you might be able to make some wonderful progress in spiritual direction or counseling. But as you notice that there is deeper work to attend to, I encourage you to deeply invest in developing the friendships you have into deeper spiritual friendships. This takes some time and some effort.

- ❖ If you do not have a spiritual director, consider finding one. (We would be happy to help. See www.orderofthecommonlife.org).
- ❖ Spend time in prayer over the next few weeks asking God to gently bring up areas in your life where you need formational healing.
- ❖ Invite some close friends, colleagues, or your spouse to be an extra set of eyes on your life. This is quite vulnerable but could be a great place to start. Ask these two questions:
  Is there a part of my story that you have wondered about but felt cautious to ask about?
  Is there any place in my life where it seems like I'm stuck?

The first question can reveal things in your story that you've only spoken a little bit about but might have those closest to you wondering if there's more there. The second offers a great opportunity for those close to you to give you some feedback about things you might not be aware of. Often our unhealed stories have a way of leaking out in our emotions.

❖ Schedule time in your calendar to pursue deeper friendship with a few spiritual friendships in your life.

❖ Make an appointment with a therapist and commit to consenting to the truth of what is there within your own story, how it has impacted you, and how the love of God might work to heal you.

For Small Groups

Processing memories, trauma, and wounds within a group can only happen if there is trust and intimacy within the group and a skilled facilitator. Take some time to linger in this section.

❖ If you haven't already shared your stories, start there. Spend a few weeks giving each person an opportunity to do this. This can build intimacy, spiritual friendship, and listening. After everyone shares, ask open-ended questions about one another's stories.

Use these prompts to help group members prepare to share:

Share something about your family of origin. What stands out to you?

What are the major moments and paths of your life?

What is currently happening in your life that feels significant?

What is something that you would like to see God do in your life?

After you spend weeks listening to one another's stories, discuss these questions.

What is God's current invitation to me toward healing the different parts of my own story?

What is God's current "workmanship" in the deepest places of my life?

Who is walking next to me in these areas?

There is no need to push people to go deeper than they feel comfortable. Simply naming out loud some of God's deeper invitations can break the silence of the hardest things in our life.

❖ Commit to one another to share, perhaps even outside of the official group time, what in your life feels like a disordered attachment. This could be a person, a substance, a specific outcome to a hard situation, or any number of things. What in your life would cause emotional instability if you didn't have access to it or it didn't pan out?

❖ Pray for one another. Remind one another of the love of God.

For Parents

I can't say it enough: parenting can stir up quite a bit from within our own stories. We watch our kids navigate the things that we had to navigate at their age. One of our kids heads off to middle school and we are suddenly thrust back into our own story. My second oldest child got her driver's license today, and all I can think about is the car wreck from more than a year ago. As our kids dip their toes into the waters of each new stage of life, sometimes what they are facing reminds us and stirs up for us those very same waters that we navigated so long ago. Anxiety around school. Perfectionism. Conflict in friendships. Feeling left out. Mental health. Physical health. Notice when the events in your child's life mirror those of your own childhood and pay attention to what this stirs up in you.

The greatest gift you can give your children is the fruit of God's healing love in your life. The opposite of this is also true, and it's quite sobering. Sometimes we know that there are parts of us that need the healing touch of God and we just can't quite seem to work through it. I have talked with parents about their fear of passing on their trauma and wounds to their kids. I am reassured, however, by watching how God generally only brings things to the surface as a way of inviting us into the healing work. If you are aware of some things that you would like God to heal, ask God for healing.

If your child is still living in your home, you can, in real time, participate in some of their healing work as it comes up. You will likely know the moments that need some extra care. Trust your instincts and follow the emotions. Get curious and help your child become curious about why the emotions are so big, for example. Or maybe their emotions seem shut down in a particular area. Each child has a different capacity to articulate their feelings. Sometimes the best thing we can do is offer a long hug during moments of deep sadness, anger, and disappointment. Here are a few other things to consider:

- ❖ Stay attuned to what your child "grabs on to." You might not even address it, but just noticing and holding it in the narrative that you have for your child will go a long way as you learn about your child.

- ❖ Remind your children occasionally that you love when they share about their life. Carve out time to demonstrate your availability without any expectation that something special will happen. Just demonstrating your presence will help create deep attachment for your child and they'll know that when they need it, you'll be there.

- ❖ In age-appropriate ways, share what God is healing in you. This will help normalize for your children the ongoing work of God in adults. Kids need to know that discipleship and formation is a partnership with God. You can help them learn this simply by living your life in front of them.

- ❖ If you haven't yet dipped into counseling, get curious about whether there are some things in your story that you are afraid to visit. What would it look like for you to consent to the truth of what is in your story?

- ❖ If you do begin counseling or therapy, don't keep it a secret. Normalize it. You don't need to talk to your children about what goes on in counseling, but let your kids know that this is a part of the way you are partnering with God's healing work in your life.

CHAPTER NINE

FAULTS
and AFFIRMATIONS

CONSENTING TO THE CONSTRAINT OF
WHAT IS TRUE

The Freedom to Walk Toward Humility

A brother in Scete happened to commit a fault, and the elders assembled, and sent for Abbot Moses to join them. He, however, did not want to come. The priest sent him a message, saying: Come, the community of the brethren is waiting for you. So he arose and started off. And taking with him a very old basket full of holes, he filled it with sand, and carried it behind him. The elders came out to meet him, and said: What is this, Father? The elder replied: My sins are running out behind me, and I do not see them, and today I come to judge the sins of another. They, hearing this, said nothing to the brother but pardoned him.

THE SAYINGS OF THE DESERT FATHERS

I t is nearly impossible to grow in the awareness of God's love for us unless we spend a great deal of time in solitude and silence. We simply must escape the noise of this world—the tweets, the constant cycle of politics, and the tidal wave of information attempting to tell us who we are. Or who we ought to be. We began the second half of this book in solitude and silence for this very reason. This is the most important practice in the journey of spiritual formation.

But it is also nearly impossible to grow into full awareness of God's love for us unless we spend time in deep community with others. We practice our spiritual training and constraints in community because God's love for us is also mediated through the people God has placed in our life. God speaks to us through Scripture, prayer, the voice of others, and the community's engagement together with the Scriptures—all empowered by the Holy Spirit.

In the practice of formational healing, we began to see that the ongoing commitment of awareness to the constraints of our own story, paired with welcoming God's light into the darkness, will almost always require the help of others. Pastors, spiritual directors, counselors, therapists, and spiritual friendships are necessary for our healing. Others are able to see in us the ongoing work of God in our lives where we cannot see it. We must have spiritual friends who are able to call out in us the beauty of God's presence and the work of God's grace in our lives. We have to have a few people in our lives who are able to both bear with us the burden of our failures and sins as well as rejoice with us in the truth of God's increasing display of Christ in our lives. We bear some responsibility to name for one another and call out in one another what we are, by grace, on our way to becoming.

This last thought is an echo of something C. S. Lewis said: "The load, or weight, or burden of my neighbor's glory should be laid daily on my back, a load so heavy that only *humility* can carry it."[1] This is the idea we're getting at as we move deeper into one another's lives through the practice of faults and affirmations—we need each other's help in order to see what is true. Getting a clear view of what is true is not always easy. We're practicing our way toward the humility required to bear the burden of one another's glory. This can only happen in vulnerable and safe community.

Consenting to the Constraint of What Is True

There are two primary tasks in the work of spiritual formation: getting a clear picture and experience of the truth of who I am and getting a clear picture and experience of the truth of who God is.[2] Most of our lives are stuck in some kind of discrepancy or conflict related to these two primary realities. (As for our view of our neighbor, I'm leaving it out for the moment, but we'll come back to it. Our view of others is mostly colored by our view of ourselves and our vision for who God is. I think the primary work of growing in a right view of others and then loving them is very much tied to our view of self. Love of neighbor is tied deeply to love of self and love of self is impossible without attention to self. Or, as Jesus put it, "Love your neighbor *as* you love yourself.")

If you are less than confident that these are the two primary issues in our formation and discipleship to Jesus, consider for a moment the current wave of deconstruction of faith sweeping the church in the United States. As the gospel story is unraveling for so many, there are few questions that people are asking that do not in the end come back to these two:

What is the truth about who I am?

What is the truth about who God is?

Much of our discipleship in the modern world has focused on the second question and given a fairly simplistic answer to the first question. We've been rightly trying to help people frame their view of God to include only what is actually *true* of God. And where people have had false views of God, and where those false views have caused them to act in error, the church has attempted to correct this *belief* about God in hopes that it will correct some behavior that is connected. Unfortunately, it just doesn't work this way. Even with all the facts about who God actually is, we do not always act accordingly. Much of the doctrinal statements of modern churches are trying to help people believe true things about God and about God's purposes in the world. We are just beginning to see that teaching people doctrine is not an adequate plan for discipleship. We need to turn our attention more to ourselves. We need to help people wrestle with the first question: *What is the truth about who I am?*

These questions are far more complex than can be addressed through a Sunday sermon series and a midweek community group. This is not meant to throw shade on the work of the church—it's simply this pastor's honest assessment of the mess that we find ourselves in. It is *true* that the storyline is falling apart for people. And while I think that both of these questions are far more complex than many of us have previously realized, practices of constraint are meant to help us on the first question. These practices of constraint are about getting an accurate view of the truth of one's own self. But why is this important?

What we desperately need in our life is an encounter between our true self and God. There is a version of our self that God is in the process of creating and then there is a version of our self that we have created. We have very much become attached to the second version, and most of us have only just begun to meet the first version.

This false version of our self lives in different "parts" of us. Here is my own confession: There is a part of me that wants this book to sell really well because that part of me craves influence and power. There is another part of me, truly, that wants this book to sell really well because I believe what I am saying could really help people. Both of these desires are true and they both feel like they are on fire someplace inside of me. The first desire is attached to some idea I have about what it means to be successful. And my idea of success and my attachment to it was developed long ago as a coping mechanism for how challenging it is to be a human. We all do this. We all have similar places and parts of us where the passions build up pressure that is ready to be released in unhelpful and unhealthy ways. For me, the pressure—for success, for the desire to be seen, and for the desire to have power—these have been building for as long as I can remember. I can see this un-healed passion at work in my life. And God is in the process of healing it.

The second desire—the one that springs from love—comes from a place in me that is on fire with the love of God. These are the two parts at work in me. One operates from the truest sense of who I am and God's love in my life, and the other operates out of my unhealed passions. All of this is happening at the same time. We are a mixed bag of competing desires. The parts of me that are excessively and inordinately attached to things contribute to what some within the contemplative tradition have called the "false self."[3]

Change can happen only when we allow God to peel back these parts of us and help us see that he is loving every single part of us toward integration as a whole *true* self. This is the encounter that we need. This is the healing of our passions, and this is how we become free.

But much of our effort toward this encounter leads us to chase after God—through study or service or even spiritual disciplines and programs. This might be hard to hear—particularly if your primary background is American evangelicalism—but the historic church bears witness that we discover the truth of who God is through the difficult work of shaving off the false layers of self in order to expose what is at the center of who *we* are. This is not to say that we should stop learning about who God is—through prayer and study and worship—but we have to give equal attention to the other question. The practices of constraint—such as solitude and silence, simplicity, marriage and celibacy, formational healing, faults and affirmations, and discernment in community—help us in this journey.

The side of the spiritual formation journey that focuses on the pursuit of the truth of one's own self is rooted in the conviction that at the center of our soul is God himself. Thomas Merton says, "You don't have to make God present to you. You make yourself present to yourself so that you know that you are in his presence . . . because he is present, and what you have to do, is to be present."[4] Augustine, speaking to God, writes, "You, however, were deeper inside me than my deepest depths and higher than my greatest heights."[5] The way that I have been imagining this and saying it in our community is that "God has stitched himself to you."

There is a truth about who you are and about who I am. We often hide what is true from one another because it is so vulnerable to let one another see the extent of our pride or lust or envy or anger or utter boredom just below the surface. Or we've pushed them all down so far that we too are unaware of them. We find it so difficult to accept ourselves and to face the reality of the truth of ourselves because we believe that these unhealed passions somehow make us unlovely. But they do not.

At the center of our soul is God, but we cannot travel to the center alone. When we attempt to face the hard truths about ourselves alone, we are also then alone with the weight of the burden of those truths. And we cannot very often bring ourselves into the loneliness of it. We need companions to help us get there. The way that we consent to the truth and bear its burden is to bring what is hidden out into the open with others who are committed to do the same in their lives. We simply say, "This is true about my life." This is the basis for the Christian practice of confession.

The challenge, of course, is finding other people who are committed to this same practice and who are committed to living it together. My hope is that by this point in the book—because you are reading it with others and are practicing together—you have at least the very beginning of the kind of spiritual friendship that can hold the humility required to bring your hidden self into the room. And when you are met with love from the people with whom you practice faults and affirmations, perhaps you might also be able to believe that the love they are loving you with *is* the love of God, mediated through his body, through the power of the Holy Spirit.

The hope for the vision laid out here, resting on the tradition of monastic communities and religious orders, is that we might become people who practice together as a way of learning the truth about ourselves and God. That we would be communities that practice with some regularity, training together (like monks and nuns and members of religious orders) in ways that help us wrestle more deeply with these two primary questions of spiritual formation.

Faults and affirmations is the practice of naming what is true about ourselves and what is true about God's work in others.

The Practice of Faults and Affirmations

"I see the way—humility; I long for the goal to which it leads—truth; but what if the way is so difficult that I can never reach the goal?" said Bernard of Clairvaux.[6] One way the monastic tradition intentionally cultivated humility was through both public and private confession. From the earliest forms of this practice we see an encouragement to pay particular attention to one's thoughts and emotions and to bring these observations into conversation with a spiritual mother or father, or a spiritual director. And if neither was available, there was a general rule that one should at least bring one's thoughts into prayer and reflection with a brother or sister.

The passions are primarily expressed in our thoughts. As we reveal our passion-infused thoughts to a trusted person, the power of those thoughts to grow into action and form us with habits is greatly diminished. We resist hiding in secret. We consent to the reality of what is true. *Yep, that thought is there. I wonder where it came from?*

There is a well-known anecdote from John Climacus, a sixth-century monk, about one of the brothers in a monastery he visited. The brother who managed the refectory (dining hall) had a small notebook hanging from a string attached to his belt. Throughout the day the brother would write down the passing thoughts in his head and bring them into prayer and confession with a superior that night. We might consider this practice too introspective and too focused on one's own self. I don't necessarily recommend the practice all the time, but it could be an interesting experiment to jot down some thoughts periodically.

What thoughts led you to sadness? What made you angry? What were you thinking about when envy rose up in you?

I have been in the habit of asking myself a handful of questions at the end of each day (through the prayer of Examen), a few questions at the end of each week, and a few at the end of each month. One of my questions at the end of each month is What are you afraid of? Over the past six or seven years, the answer to this question has remained almost entirely the same, though the strength of the fear has lessened substantially. I am more or less afraid of the same things I was afraid of eight years ago, but there has been a tremendous degree of healing and those fears which once occupied more of me are now there only as residue. Dust. I haven't always practiced this consistently, and for some long stretches, not at all. But the limited follow-through has yielded some fruit. I've had the same spiritual director for most of the last decade, and we can now see that the pattern of thoughts is well embedded and is slowly being healed by the grace and love of God. But without the commitment to revealing them through confession my life would look very different.

This individualized practice of revealing thoughts among the early monks was eventually brought into community through the Rule of Saint Benedict. The tradition that emerged from the Rule is called the "chapter of faults"—a gathering of the community to hear a public confession of faults against the community's rule. Private thoughts were still confessed privately to a spiritual director, but public actions that impacted the entire community or offenses toward another brother could be shared publicly.

Say, for example, you were late for prayer (or slept through it altogether) or failed to do the work assigned to you in the garden. Or say you were in a hurry in your task and broke a bowl in the kitchen. You could clear your conscience of the faults that impacted the community in front of the community. But this wasn't for the sake of keeping score or a record of wrongs, at least not when it was practiced with Benedict's intention in view. This practice was so that whenever you committed a fault that impacted the community (like arriving late to morning prayer), you could simply notice what everyone else was already aware of (you were late). From our vantage point this might feel a bit legalistic, and there is a danger that it could become so. But this confession was always voluntary. This was a community full of trust. And they were all committed to intentionally forming humility.

This practice was a simple way of combating pride and leveling out the power within a community. If everyone is freely sharing the ways they have failed on this particular day or week, whatever shame culture might exist (which is really a culture of pride) is eventually eradicated because there is no reward in hiding one's faults. Nobody is keeping score. Whatever illusion one might have of being better than another melts away because the community is practicing a radical acceptance of the truth of one another.

There is a section of Rumor Godden's novel of monastic life, *In This House of Brede,* where the nuns comment on this practice:

> The Chapter of Faults had the effect of welding the nuns together and making them like one another. "You can't be afraid of someone, even as sharp and clever as Dame Agnes," said Cecily, "when you have seen her keel down before us all, even us young ones she teaches, and say,

'Three times yesterday I said things that cut,' or 'I lost my temper.' Especially when you know you will probably lose yours tomorrow," said Hilary.[7]

Before we take a deeper look at how the practices of confession of faults and the blessing of others through affirmations help us get to the truth about who we are and who God is, let me share how this has worked in the life of our family. This practice does not need to feel heavy or demanding. In fact, we've found a lot of joy and laughter in it over the years. The goal is not constant self-evaluation but creating a culture where mistakes and failure are normalized. We'll get really practical in the final pages of this chapter—for now, here is a little peek.

We began the practice of faults and affirmations in our home around 2015. Our kids were eleven, ten, eight, and five years old. We started around the dinner table about once a week, and it took months to catch on and more than a year of occasional (flexible) practice to become a part of our life. This practice allowed us to normalize being humans making human mistakes and to be a family where it is okay to fail. Forgiveness and grace were always available. We would often begin with a simple invitation, "Let's do faults and affirmations tonight." The ground rules were clear: you can only share a fault about yourself, and you could only share an affirmation about another. I would usually begin with something like this to set the pace: "Girls, I just want to recognize that I spoke harshly out of frustration yesterday and raised my voice. I'm really sorry about this, please forgive me."

Other times my wife, Jaime, and I would just notice out loud that we had mistreated each other in some way. Much of the conflict in our marriage in the years when our kids were little happened along the way of living life—unloading groceries, budgeting, and keeping our house intact. We didn't have the luxury of always arguing in secret. We were almost always with our kids as conflict and disagreement broke out. This means that our impatience with one another, our anger and pride and lack of gentleness, often occurred with our kids present. They've seen us have conflict and they've seen us work through it. They have seen us frustrated and angry with one another. We decided to live real life in front of our kids.

What this means is that our faults, in the context that I am describing, were public, at least within our household. And one of the assumptions that we've tried to integrate into the practice of faults and affirmations is that public offenses can be confessed publicly. It's never required, but we've tried to model it: "Girls, I spoke unkindly to Momma this morning after breakfast. I've already asked for her forgiveness, but I also wanted to let you know that I'm sorry for my unkindness."

Almost every time in those early years of practice, when I would confess a fault, my girls would all say, "We forgive you, Daddy." This has been a training ground for humility in my life.

Affirmations are equally powerful. As we ate dinner we created space for anyone to say, "I have a fault" or "I have an affirmation!"

"I have an affirmation for Momma! Momma, thank you for taking us to the park today."

"Dad, thank you for reading *The Hobbit* to me."

Creating space for intentional affirmations helps us practice noticing the good in others.

Over the years the intentional practice of faults and affirmations in a specific context (once a week at dinner) has helped us train our muscles of confession and blessing. Because we practiced it at a specific time and place, we are now able to freely practice it at any time and at any place. Asking for forgiveness and noticing the graces that we see in one another has become very natural. And, as we have all matured, the depth of the noticing has matured as well.

Three of our kids are now teenagers and they are fairly quick to ask for forgiveness when tempers run hot or when hitting the snooze button too many times makes everyone late for school. It takes more intentionality to create space for affirmations, but when we do, it too comes quite naturally. We offer frequent affirmations and blessings, and none of it seems out of place. While we've never said this explicitly, we have consented to the truth that we are both sinners and saints. Father Jacque Philippe writes,

> The freedom to be sinners doesn't mean we are free to sin without worrying about the consequences—that would not be freedom but irresponsibility. It means we are not crushed by the fact of being sinners—we have a sort of "right" to be poor, the right to be what we are. . . . It gives us the "right to make mistakes," and delivers us, so to speak, from the imprisoning sense that we ought to be something other than we are.[8]

How does the practice of faults and affirmations train us in humility? How does this practice help us see the truth of who we are and the truth of who God is?

Faults: The Practice of Seeing the Truth in Us

"Therefore confess your sins to each other and pray for each other so that you may be healed" (Jas 5:16). When we commit to see the truth of who we are, we eventually learn to entrust ourselves into the hands of God and into the hands of our brothers and sisters. This is a radical trust in God that bends us toward humility. Confessing our private thoughts to another (a spiritual friend or a spiritual director) and our public faults to those our faults impacted publicly (within a family, roommates, a staff team) is meant to get us in touch with the love and the grace of God. And when we are met with grace for the faults we have become aware of, we also can begin to learn the grace of God for whatever hidden thoughts or sins or faults that we are not yet attentive to.

I don't think we entirely leave behind a practice of *being attentive to ourselves*, but practicing confession eventually helps free us from so much focus on whether or not we're "doing it right"—whatever "it" might be. Once we gain clarity about the truth of the shadow side of ourselves (that part we want to hide) we learn that even that shadow side is loved by God. And, when we get acquainted to this degree with the love of God, we learn to entrust all of our self—even the shadow side—into the care of God. We are set at ease knowing that we are not, in the end, responsible to heal those faults. We confess and pray and then, as James writes, the healing comes to us within the practice of confession and prayer.

Augustine writes,

No one among humankind knows what it is to be a human being, unless that human's spirit within himself knows; *but there is nevertheless something in a human being that not even the spirit within himself knows.* You, however, know everything about him, because you made him. . . . Therefore I will testify to what I know and don't know about myself, because you give me the light by which to know what I know; and

what I don't know, I don't know only until my darkness becomes as bright as noon in the light of your face before me.[9]

We learn humility first by consenting to the truth of what we
find within us, and then we learn a greater degree of humility in
realizing that there are still parts of us that we have yet to explore—
wounds and faults and sins we cannot see and thus cannot confess,
but God can see them. This next level of humility is one that
learns to trust that God is even loving the parts of us that we are
unaware of. If God loves you and accepts you in all the seen and
unseen places in your life, should you not also? What this radical
consent to the truth does to us is it leads us to a place where we
rest in the love of God. And we slowly and quietly begin to think
less often of our *self*—and this frees us up to think more often of
others. What we learn about the truth of who God is through
confession is that God is loving every part of us at every time. We
learn that he is trustworthy.

Affirmations: The Practice of Seeing the Truth in Others

In many ways it will be hard to see and say something about the
good in others unless we have settled into the fact—consented in
our own hearts—that we are not better than others. This is what I
take to be the main idea of Jesus' invitation to imagine our own
faults as a wood plank in our eye and the faults of another as a tiny
speck. Tending to the wood plank in our own eye will be necessary for us to even begin to see properly. This means that until
we have done the work of the confession of faults, we will be
unable to see clearly. Our view of others is colored by our view of
ourselves. And if we haven't yet done this work of looking at

ourselves, we will not yet have come into contact with the radical grace and love of God.

Jesus is saying, "Look at your own faults and you will see clearly to look at your neighbor's faults." But the implication is that once you do the work of seeing that your own faults obscure your vision of the other (represented by a wood plank), you will also be able to see that the faults of your brother or sister or neighbor are now suddenly quite small. I don't think Jesus is actually saying our neighbor has fewer faults than we have. I think he's saying that our vision is going to be obstructed unless we first take an inventory and are able, through reflection and confession, to consent to the truth about our own faults. This will naturally produce in us a little humility. And once we are humbled by our own faults and sin and weakness, I think we become less concerned about the faults of others.

The practice of affirmations is the practice of blessing others with our voice and our body and our presence in ways that call out and notice the good in the other.

I noticed that you have been taking risks in your leadership recently—I think God is growing courage in you.

I see the work you are putting into hosting others in your home— it's really beautiful. I would love to hear from you how this feels for you as you take those risks.

I've seen you laugh a lot recently—I see the joy in your life.

I've watched you grow in kindness and patience over this past year—this has really made a difference in our team.

This kind of intentionality trains us toward humility in several ways.

First, it trains our attention toward noticing the good in others. What prevents us from blessing others is mostly pride and a lack of attention to others. We can't affirm others if we are not paying attention to the beautiful work of God in them. And we cannot pay attention to that beautiful work if we are so focused on ourselves that we are unable to truly see the work of God in the other. If pride is a version of self-focus, then training ourselves away from pride and toward humility means that we will first be attentive to our faults. We get a clear view of ourselves and God's love, and *then* we are able to see others with the truth that we have learned in the practice of confession: God loves me. And if God is loving me, both in the places I can see and in those I cannot see in myself, then I can trust that God is also loving this person in front of me. He is loving them in the tangible things of their life that I can see as well as in the places I cannot see.

Second, it combats the passions of envy and pride. We not only consent to what is true in our own life with the practice of faults, but in the practice of affirmations we also consent to what is true about others. There are people who are more gifted than I am. There are people who practice their craft in ways that maybe stir up something in us—they're a better preacher, or teacher, or musician. Consenting to the truth of this reality, blessing them in the gifts they hold and the grace of God in their lives reminds us that every good thing comes from God. If someone is more gifted than we are at something, or has more favor than we do in an area of life, affirming them is a way of saying to ourselves, "I do not need to be anything other than what I am." We have the portion of gifts that God has given us. Others have the portion that God has given them. In the end, all are gifts from God for the building up of his body, the church. This helps us lean into the exhortation that Paul gives in 1 Corinthians 12.

Third, we learn to entrust the work of noticing the good in ourselves to others. When we are in a community of people who are freely sharing their faults and struggles through the practice of both private and public confession, and when those same people are also freely affirming the good in one another, we grow in humility because we can stop worrying about whether or not the good in us will be noticed and seen by others. With the practice of faults and affirmations, the good in me *is* being noticed by others and I am hearing about it.

I think we do not have enough of a culture of noticing and naming the good we see in others. We are much more acquainted with work cultures and family cultures where the things we do wrong are pointed out but the places where we are flourishing are less noticed. At the very least successes are less often verbalized than criticism unless a culture of celebration and affirmation is being created intentionally. But we can change this by showing up with a focus on noticing and naming the good in others. It will help others see the good in themselves in ways they may not have seen before. We help them see the truth of themselves.

The Freedom to Walk Toward Humility

To return to Benedict's ladder of humility, the journey of the spiritual life, at its essence, is a journey toward humility. It's a journey away from self-sufficiency and toward the sufficiency of God's love. What I hope is slowly becoming clear is that we often need others to help us see all the parts of us that God loves. This happens when we bring our faults to others and receive grace and forgiveness. This happens too when we are in a community that can see the good in us and affirm it as the goodness of God. The freedom that the practice of faults and affirmations is meant to bring to us is the freedom to learn to walk in the state of humility.

If you were to go read the Rule of Saint Benedict and begin working your way through chapter seven of the rule, you would find twelve "steps" on the ladder of humility (sometimes referred to as "degrees of humility"). We might stumble over some of the language and implications of Benedict's teaching about humility. We have to remember that Benedict lived at a very different time, and much of what he is writing requires some commentary to bridge the fifteen-hundred-year gap between then and now.[10] In many ways the entire history of this tradition has been a living commentary on Benedict's Rule.

Benedict's steps of humility are meant to be signposts that one might notice along the journey. They are not tests on an obstacle course that we can master or work through. The spirit of the degrees of humility is to simply help a brother or sister living in a community notice where God's work in them is coming to fruition. I don't think we need to use Benedict's ladder to measure our humility (I'm not a Benedictine), but it is a helpful metaphor. We do not *climb* a ladder of humility; we are led along it by the grace of God and then we notice that something in our life has shifted. We've progressed in some way, but the progress was primarily God's progress in us.

The fifth degree of humility, for example, is when we have the willingness to not keep any secret thought hidden from a trusted spiritual guide. For those following Benedict's Rule, this guide was most often the abbot or abbess, or perhaps a spiritual director. If you do not have a trusted spiritual friend or spiritual director, it will be difficult for you to intentionally open yourself up to God's work of humility in community. You might find the idea of fully confessing all your secrets to a spiritual director or a spiritual friend an occasion for shame. Perhaps the mere thought of doing this makes you shrink back. This, I think, is normal.

What eventually happens on the road of formation is that the shame goes away as we partner with the grace of God. It doesn't go away because we try to climb that particular rung of the humility ladder and finally accomplish it. We notice one day that our shame is gone. Or at least enough of it is gone that we can tell one person who loves and cares for us absolutely every wayward and sinful thought. This is how the ladder of humility is meant to work.

A signpost a little further down the ladder is being able to walk into a room and immediately see the good in others in a way that disposes us toward loving them. Our gaze is so trained and fixed on our role in seeing the good in others that we almost stop thinking about ourselves in comparison. This, at least, is my own interpretation and application of the seventh degree of humility. It reminds me of Jesus' teaching about the dinner guests who picked out the places of honor at the table:

> When someone invites you to a wedding feast, do not take the place of honor, for a person more distinguished than you may have been invited. If so, the host who invited both of you will come and say to you, "Give this person your seat." Then, humiliated, you will have to take the least important place. But when you are invited, take the lowest place, so that when your host comes, he will say to you, "Friend, move up to a better place." Then you will be honored in the presence of all the other guests. For all those who exalt themselves will be humbled, and those who humble themselves will be exalted. (Lk 14:8-11)

The only way that someone can take the place of honor when they walk into a room is if they are thinking of themselves. They think of their own place in the room and decide, "I deserve to sit near the head of the table." But, if we train ourselves to see the good in others, we will quite naturally recognize that they have so much good in them that perhaps *they* are the guests of honor. Our enthusiasm for ourselves might be particularly tempered if we are in touch with our faults and the parts of ourselves operating to push up the false self.

This whole affair might set us up in a trap of comparison, but this too pushes us in the opposite direction of humility. Comparison is a truth killer. Depending on our particular unhealed passion our view of ourselves and others will either be too puffed up or too negative. Both of these are a trap. In the end, humility births in us a sense of rest in God's love such that we do not need to compare ourselves to others. We have a true view of our self before God and a true view of others before God. The practice of faults and affirmations nurtures both of these views. And this on-going work gives us the freedom to walk *intentionally* toward humility, where we can freely be honest about our own shortcomings and about the good work of God in others.

In the end, the journey toward humility is always wrapped up in our capacity to see and take in the *truth* of the way things are— in us and in others. And when we are on this journey we are also growing in love because love, as a concrete action, requires that we look out for the interests of others above our own interests. We think of others, as the apostle Paul instructs, "as more important than ourselves." We become like Abbot Moses who, when invited to bring accusation against another brother, is so aware that there are faults of his own that he cannot yet see—they're leaking out of him like sand through a well-worn basket—he can't imagine bringing judgment against another.[11]

PRACTICING
FAULTS AND AFFIRMATIONS

For Pastors and Leaders

This particular practice of constraint might be the easiest one to implement in your leadership team. If you are on staff at a local church, you can immediately begin to cast some vision for making this a part of your team's weekly or monthly rhythm. Here are a few practical suggestions to get you started.

❖ If the people on your team are reading this book, you're all set to begin. If you have people on your team who are not reading this book, introduce the practice of faults and affirmations with a brief explanation. Share an example of a fault that may have impacted the team. For example,

Last week I didn't prepare well for our team meeting and the meeting didn't go well.

I haven't been living into my own practice of rest and sabbath recently, and I think I've been pushing us all too hard.

I have an affirmation for Samantha—you led well last week from up front. You sounded so clear in the vision you were casting.

❖ Choose a season of three to six months where you put faults and affirmations on your meeting agenda with regularity. This could be weekly or monthly but give it some time to work its way into the culture of your team and do it in a way that people are expecting it. Some people will need some time to think ahead. Encouraging people to come prepared to practice faults and affirmations will create some safety in the room.

❖ If you do not have a spiritual director or spiritual friend with whom you can reveal everything—this can be the next step.

What do you notice about yourself as you share your own faults with your team?

What is your experience of watching people on your team have the courage to share their own failures?

❖ Spend some time reflecting and journaling how this practice is changing and shaping the culture of your team. Invite others on your team to do this as well. Taking a step back and naming how this work is changing the dynamic is important.

How easy is it to affirm others on your team?

How are others experiencing the affirmation?

How are you experiencing the affirmation of others?

For Small Groups

This practice will best work in a group of people who have already created safety in relationships. If your group hasn't spent a lot of time together, perhaps hold off on this practice until you have gotten to know one another a little more. Here are some ideas to get you started:

❖ If the people in your group are reading this book, you're all set to begin. Just choose a time to come together to practice this. If you have people in your group who are not reading this book, introduce the practice of faults and affirmations with a brief explanation. Share an example of a fault that might be meaningful to the group. This could be an appropriate fault or failing from your life outside of the group, but share something that would be appropriate to the group context. A general confession in a group of people is not what we're looking for here. But, if you've been struggling with anger, or you've noticed yourself distancing from others—say this out loud!

❖ You might consider beginning with a night of affirmations. This is usually a little easier in a group that isn't quite ready to dive deeper. The important part of this practice is that whatever you say needs to be *real*. Don't make up an affirmation just to make someone feel good—that will lessen the impact all around.

❖ Cultivate a time of silence and ask God to help the group notice the work that he is doing in others. *We're going to begin in silence and we're going to ask God to bring to our attention the slow and steady work he is doing in one another.*
What did this practice do within the group?

❖ Jot down some tangible things that you noticed after the first intentional practice of faults and affirmations. Encourage others in this noticing practice. Revisit this work of noticing together after the group has practiced this for a season (maybe once a month for six months). Thank God for the graces.

For Parents

I've already written in this chapter how we have practiced faults and affirmations in our home. You may need to adjust the practice to the rhythms of your home and to the needs of your family. Maybe doing this around the dinner table is not the best idea. Maybe for your family an after-dinner walk is best, or maybe everyone sitting on the floor in the family room is better. Experiment for a season.

❖ Begin by introducing the idea of making faults and affirmations part of the rhythm of your family. Talk about forgiveness as something that we need to practice just like we practice learning an instrument or making an omelet.

❖ Lead by example. Do your first practice of faults and affirmations when you know that you have something to confess or make right with someone. If you lost your patience today and got angry—this is the day to start this practice. Use your own life as a parent as the first example. *I spoke unkindly today. Please forgive me.*

❖ Make it full of affirmations! It's important that every time we engage in this practice people feel the joy of affirmations more than the pain of faults. Both faults and affirmations can be age appropriate.

❖ For younger kids, notice and affirm things like joy, playfulness, expressions of love and kindness. It's fine to also affirm the things they do but look to affirm the things that might not be as obvious. It's easy to affirm your kids when they have done a good job at a task or accomplished something. They should be affirmed for this. But try to go one step deeper and affirm in them what others in their life might not be able to see.

❖ Affirm older kids and teens in what you see developing in their character. For example: *I noticed that you had a hard conversation with your teacher yesterday. That took a lot of courage—I love that you are courageous.* Teenagers are in a season of trying to figure out who they are. They need to be affirmed in those hard-to-see places.

❖ Don't shy away from confessing the hard relationship stuff or the hard personal stuff—particularly with older kids. There are a lot of misunderstandings between parents and teenagers especially. *I'd like to share a fault. I notice that recently we've really missed each other in conversation, and I know I've jumped to some conclusions. I'm really sorry about this. Please forgive me for not listening more deeply to what you are trying to say.*
I have a fault I'd like to share. I think I've been working too much. I've been feeling anxious and sometimes when I feel anxious I keep myself busy. I know this isn't good for me or our family—I'm really sorry. Please forgive me.

CHAPTER TEN

DISCERNMENT
in COMMUNITY

CONSENTING TO THE CONSTRAINTS OF
ONE ANOTHER

The Freedom to Trust

The peace which Christ brings is not a formula for individual
peace, nor for egotistical self-fulfillment. There can be no peace
in the heart of the man who seeks peace for himself alone. To
find true peace, peace in Christ, we must desire others to have
peace as well as ourselves, and we must be willing to sacrifice
something of our own peace and happiness in order that
others may have peace, and that others may be happy.

THOMAS MERTON

Do nothing out of selfish ambition or vain conceit. Rather, in
humility value others above yourselves, not looking to your
own interests but each of you to the interests of the others.

PHILIPPIANS 2:4

n the opening chapter of the Rule of Saint Benedict we learn that Benedict is not opposed to throwing a little shade. He opens his "little rule for beginners" by describing four kinds of monks, though the way that he describes them, it is not difficult to see ourselves and our own church communities in them.

Benedict makes clear from the very beginning that he has one particular kind of person in mind—the kind that is living in *community* and allowing their life to be shaped by others. This is the first kind of monk he describes and the one we might most often imagine, living in a monastery with a life shaped by prayer and chores and the annoying habits of one's brothers or sisters.

The second kind of monk is those who have *already* allowed their life to be radically shaped by community. They've lived the communal life for years. They have learned how to be with people in a way that preferences the other, serves the other, makes room for the other's way. They have learned how to not only look out for their own interests, as the apostle Paul instructs. They've learned the long lesson of also looking out for the interests of others.

Then Benedict throws shade on two additional kinds of monks who claim to live a life of ascetic constraint but do so in a way that feels false and misleading.

The first group he criticizes he calls "detestable." These are the Sarabaites. They do not live by a shared set of common commitments, they are not loyal to one another (but rather to the world), and they do whatever they want to do. "Anything they believe in and choose, they call holy; anything they dislike, they consider forbidden."[1] Sister Aquanata Böckmann writes in her commentary on the Rule of Benedict about the spirit of the Sarabaites, which also very much lives in us:

There is also a tendency in each of us not to expose ourselves to criticism and to challenging questions. The Sarabaites define their . . . life along their own views, and their
own interpretation is their norm. They see hardly any need
to listen to the experience of others or to accept spiritual
direction in order to learn from the wisdom of others. "I
already know what I have to do," they might say. Thus they
can build a fence around themselves and lock themselves
up inside.[2]

In short—they have no hearth or furnace of community in order
to make them burn hot.

The second group is worse than the first. Benedict calls them
Gyrovagues. They spend their lives drifting around, receiving the
hospitality of different kinds of communities but they never settle
down. They go from one community to another. Benedict writes
that they "are slaves to their own wills and gross appetites."[3]

Benedict makes clear, on the opening pages of his manifesto,
that we can only be formed in community. He had nothing to say
to men and women who did not want to be shaped by others. He
simply wrote them off. The only way that humans can change is
through giving and receiving love. And this is not something you
can do apart from allowing your life to be constrained by others.

When we give love, what is really happening is that we are responding to a need or desire in another person. We are seeing
them. We are choosing to act on their behalf, and this attunement
to another also does something *in us*. It nurtures us toward humility. In loving another we are drawn away from exercising our
will to serve ourselves and toward exercising our will for the sake
of someone else.

We also learn humility when we allow ourselves to receive love because when we receive love we are consenting to the fact that we do not have everything that we need. Being loved means allowing someone else to act upon us. "We need to be acted upon by others."[4]

Benedict threw shade at individualism because the only change agent for humans is *love*.

The surrender of one's will for the sake of others—this creates real heat. It's why community is a furnace. And it is the only possible context where we can become "all flame." If we are unattached to others in a way that others are not able to make real demands on our lives, then we are in danger of never having the opportunity to love or be loved. These real demands don't have to be actual demands that others voice to us. Simply being in a relationship with others will make demands on us. In the natural course of our life together we will be given the opportunity to relinquish our own way and act with a love that considers others' interests above our own. Seeing the way that we might love others fans small sparks of love within us. And when we act in love for another, when we allow our life to be constrained by others' needs and desires, those small sparks of love become flames.

The practice of discernment in community intentionally invites others to speak into our lives and decisions. It requires us to consent to the constraints that others' ideas and opinions and needs might place on us. This practice nurtures mutuality and brings us toward a freedom to entrust our lives into the care of others. Ultimately, this is a way of entrusting our lives into God's care.

The Practice of Discernment in Community

Benedict writes, "Listen carefully . . . to the master's instructions, and attend to them with the ear of your heart." The first word of the prologue to the Rule of Life is the word *listen*. It frames everything that follows. "The master" is Christ himself, and the seventy-two chapters that follow are primarily meant to help members of Benedict's communities learn how to listen carefully. The rhythms of prayer and study and work and rest are all designed to create a container, a *life*, so that the ear of our heart can become attuned to the master's voice. This life of listening can only happen in community.

The practice of discernment "recognize[s] and respond[s] to the presence and activity of God—both in the ordinary moments and in the larger decisions of our lives."[5] This is how Ruth Haley Barton describes discernment in her excellent manual for the practice of group discernment. Discernment in community means that we're doing the work of noticing and nurturing the presence of God's activity with and for one another. Discernment seems to be the apex of what it means to walk in a way of life that is committed to listening. Being able to recognize and respond to the presence of God is to join Christ in "seeing what the Father is doing" and joining him on this path.

Discernment for our own life. There are two primary modes of discernment in community. First of all, we invite a group of people around us to help us find our way and to *listen* through some of the larger decisions of our lives. This is discernment for *our own life*.

These are decisions like getting married, moving to a different city, maybe taking a new job or shifting one's vocational path. I had a group of people around me, for example, that helped me discern whether to take on this book project. We asked some deeper questions together like, "Why do I want to write this book?" "Do I have time for it?" "How will it impact my other work? My family? My margins?" I was able to say to this group, "If you see something that I cannot see, please don't hesitate to let me know." Choosing to write a book might not seem like a large decision, but I knew it would impact a lot of other areas of my life.

In my church community, we have helped people discern moving to a new city, leaning into a pastoral calling, stepping away from pastoral ministry, starting a nonprofit, and navigating some larger financial decisions. We helped a group of single adults discern moving into a house together. In all of these examples (and there are dozens more) we've been able to gather around people in these moments to help them see clearly what is at stake in their decision, what is at work within them that has the fingerprint of God on it, and what might be holding them back from saying yes to God's invitations.

The inner work required from everyone involved is extraordinary to watch unfold. These bigger decisions have a way of pushing things to the surface that otherwise may never have emerged. There are often tears of pain as fear or pride or loss surfaces in the presence of others when our life gets "stirred up" by big decisions. But there are also often tears of joy and those particular tears that come when you feel loved and supported in ways that you didn't know you needed.

I do not believe that we are meant to make these kinds of life-altering decisions alone. We only believe that we are supposed to make these decisions alone because we have a particular view of freedom that is untethered from *mutuality* in relationships. We believe that we have the capacity to see more clearly than we are actually able to see. And we believe that, if we cannot see clearly in the present moment, this is due to some deficiency in *ourselves*. But our own limits, again, are not a flaw; they are a feature. From the opening scenes of the Scriptures we see that it is not good for the human to be alone. Why would we consider it good for us to sort out by ourselves some of the most challenging and impactful decisions of our lives? The weight is too much to bear. And when we try to bear the weight of these decisions alone and make these decisions from our own perspective without the aid of the community that God has given us, we deny others an opportunity to be involved in bearing the burden with us. And when we do this, we also deny them the opportunity to join Christ in his mission to fulfill what the law was always meant to do—to teach us to love as God loves.[6] Christian community is meant to be a place to hold these decisions within a sacred process of listening carefully together for one another.

Discernment for our life together. The second mode of discernment pertains to decisions that need to be made for a community (church, team, family). This is discernment for our *life together*.

Discernment within a group *for* a group also requires a deep commitment to listening carefully. In group discernment everyone shows up with their own perspective, prayerfully, to see what might emerge as the way forward when we each bring our own gifts into the community. We rest on the assumption that no one person has everything that they need. As much as we wish to be self-sufficient, we are not. We are designed for mutuality and interdependence. We are the body of Christ, who is the head. And, as Paul reminds us, each member in the body has a role to play. This doesn't mean that everyone's perspective has equal weight. The role of the leader or leaders within a group is to lead. But this doesn't mean that the leader is always the decision maker. It might be the case that when everyone brings what they have to the group discernment process, an impasse is reached and an agreement about a decision doesn't initially emerge. We take a step back and reconsider. A leader could, as part of her own discernment process, appoint someone else in the group to make the final decision.

In healthy communities the *process* of discernment is even more important than the outcome. It is the process of inviting everyone who is part of the discernment process to pray, to speak up, to advocate, to argue, and disagree. Then a healthy community with a healthy process can entrust authority to a smaller group of people to make a final decision. The real challenge to discernment in community *for* the community is that often the best way forward will not serve everyone's interests equally.

Again, we have an opportunity in discernment to become aware of what is at work in our own inner life. What passions might be causing so much frustration or attachment to getting our own way? The formational space that group discernment provides sums up much of the work we've been doing in this book. The constraints provided through the process become an agitator for the unhealed passions to leak out in places where we can then pay deeper attention to them. Mostly this is due to the possibility that we will not get our way, which feels threatening to our individuality.

The outcome of a discerned decision is not the final product of the process of discernment. The decision is, of course, part of the purpose of the practice of discernment in community, but a greater goal within the discernment process is to become the kind of community that is able to love one another well and to listen together. In every group discernment, nearly everyone is faced with moments of self-surrender and giving up their own way for the sake of the community as a whole. This is sacred. It's what the church can uniquely do in the world. And our ability to do this, even within the midst of disagreement, is how others learn that our faith in Christ is authentic (Jn 13:35).

Becoming a Community of Discernment

If you are looking to become a community who can do the work of discernment together or you want to build a community that can practice together—there are some very practical resources to help you. I'll offer a road map for how to begin to pursue this way of life, but there are other resources that can help you once you have gathered those committed to becoming the kind of people who can do this work together.[7]

What I will lay out here is the inner work that this practice requires and the freedom from the unhealed passions of pride and the accompanying self-protection that pursuing discernment within community can reveal to us.

In many ways, the work we have been doing through the previous practices has already started us on the journey toward the practice of discernment within community. You may have noticed that we began our practices of constraint with the most individualized practice (solitude and silence) and are ending with the most communal. All the work we've done in between has slowly been moving us deeper into community and growing our capacity to allow others to contribute to our process of listening. All the literature I have read on what it means to be a community of discernment and mutuality agrees on one basic beginning: in order to become a community of discernment we must have individuals who are committed to becoming the kind of people who can listen.

This doesn't mean that everyone needs to be an expert in noticing the presence of God. But everyone does at least need to be committed to growing in freedom from unhealed passions.

It will be difficult, for example, to hear input from our community about financial decisions we need to make from those who are not aware of the hold that wealth and possessions might have on their own life.

It will make discernment for the community difficult if those doing the discernment work have not also attended to parts of their own stories that cause them to show up in the room with a great deal of fear. How will the group decide to move in a risky decision? How will the group help me navigate a risky decision if many of its members have a disordered attachment to security?

How will someone pursue a process of discernment around a calling to marriage or singleness within a community that idolizes marriage or does not have the imagination for a life without sexual intimacy?

One of the first steps of discernment for the medium-sized and bigger decisions in our life is gathering all the facts that bear upon the decision being made. But certainly some of the "facts" that bear upon the decision might be our own inner fears and emotional processes—things that we are afraid to share for fear of judgment. The practice of faults and affirmations can prepare the way here. If we have practiced confessing our faults and weaknesses in community already, we can bring everything relevant to a decision into the process without fearing judgment from those who are helping us discern because we know that in this community we are loved and the people loving us have also shared their own struggles.

At the very least, for discernment within community to be possible, everyone will need to be committed to the pursuit of humility. We must be committed to being aware of our weaknesses and limitations in order for discernment to take root. Otherwise, we'll never seek out others' input and perspective.

One of the first examples of communal discernment we have from the early church is reported in Acts 15, the story of the Jerusalem Council. The main question at hand was whether or not new Gentile converts would be required to adhere to Jewish laws and customs like circumcision. Some from Judea were saying, "Absolutely! You have to be circumcised to be saved." But Paul and Barnabas felt differently, and it was decided that Paul and Barnabas go to seek council with the elders and apostles in Jerusalem. After much debate Peter spoke up and gave his own argument, and then Paul and Barnabas added in their perspective based on what *they* had seen among the Gentiles who had not been circumcised: God was doing signs and wonders among them! James spoke up and offered his own thoughts leveraging the voices of the prophets.

In the end, the council decided on three things that the Gentiles needed to abstain from "food polluted by idols, from sexual immorality, from the meat of strangled animals and from blood" (Acts 15:20). They wrote a letter to the churches in Antioch and Syria and Cilicia to communicate their discerned decision. The most striking thing about the whole process of discernment is the way that Luke reports how it *felt* for the apostle and elders once they reached a conclusion. He said, "It *seemed* good" (Acts 15:22), and later, "It *seemed* good to the Holy Spirit and to us." They had a discussion, but they communicated with humility. *We are not certain about this, but it seems to be the best direction.*

Discernment rarely ends in certainty because if the matter were so certain there would probably be no need for discernment. In the absence of certainty, we can take refuge in humility. So often when we are experiencing weakness and limitations, we try to escape those feelings. We craft our understanding of our situation in a way that makes us feel like we have a handle on it. But there is a great refuge to be found *within* that feeling of weakness and limitation. We can settle into a deeper awareness that we can only see in part—again, our weakness and the help of God.

Humility is also necessary in discernment within a community because there is some measure of self-surrender in bringing your full self into the process of discernment. *What if I share my perspective and the group discerns a different direction? What if I need to make a decision for my own life and someone I love and trust offers a word of caution or expresses a concern about something I've said?* When we come into community, we give up our self in some small measure.

A Story of Discernment in Community

In the spring of 2021 we hosted an international student from our girls' high school for a week. Ellie was living with another family that had gone on vacation and the school asked us to host her for a week. While she was staying with us, we got to hear some of her story of growing up in China and coming to the United States for high school. She hadn't been home in over three years. The Covid pandemic had prevented her from making the trip back to China in 2020, and given the hefty travel restrictions during that time, her mother could not travel to the United States.

When Ellie left at the end of the week, our oldest daughter shared with us that after some late-night conversations with Ellie, she thought we should consider hosting Ellie for her senior year. Our daughter told us that she had been praying about it for a couple of days. My first thought internally was *oh . . . I'm glad you are praying!* We listened to our daughter's reasoning and asked her a few questions about what it *felt* like when she prayed about this. We were open to considering it but given our Covid-weariness and the fact there were already six of us in the house, I honestly didn't think it was something that we would in the end give a "thumbs up" to.

What I didn't know yet was that while Ellie was with us for that week, my wife, Jaime, had also had the passing thought that perhaps we should host Ellie for her senior year. Ellie and Jaime had a few conversations that made Jaime wonder if there was something our family was meant to be a part of in Ellie's life. Over dinner a few days after our daughter brought this to us, Jaime told me that as she had prayed about our daughter's idea she noticed that something was stirring in her as well.

The idea of inviting another person into our home was the furthest thing from my mind. We didn't have another bedroom for her. I already felt at my parenting capacity with four kids. Ellie was almost eighteen but was still navigating a lot of decisions like college applications and living with the reality that it would be some time before she could see her parents. Jaime and I decided not to have the conversation with the rest of our family unless the school called and asked us to consider hosting her.

Two weeks later the school reached out to us to see if we would host Ellie for the 2021–2022 school year. We had never mentioned to them that this had come to mind for us, and we didn't know that they had been wondering for nearly a month where Ellie would spend her senior year. With all the evidence pointing in this direction we could have immediately replied with our yes, but we didn't need to hurry. We slowed the process down and noted that at the very least this could be a great opportunity for us to teach our kids about group discernment.

So we began to talk about this possibility with our other kids. There was some resistance, as expected, given that our house already felt fairly full. We spent about a week or so revisiting this with each of our kids, giving them space to share their concerns. We all imagined what it could be like to move forward, and we each noted how it *felt* to live into this possibility. We received a little more information from the school and learned that the basement bedroom that we had for Ellie would not work out. Because it was not technically up to code for a bedroom, Ellie would not be allowed to sleep there. We thought at first that this was a closed door, but then our oldest again came to us and said, "It's just for ten months—I can move downstairs and Ellie can have my room." There's something about the way that this unfolded that caught my attention. I honestly was not feeling great about hosting. But what I wanted more was to do my best to follow our oldest daughter's lead. I didn't want to get in the way of something that she was sensing—something that she could see that I couldn't quite yet see.

After a few more days of consideration we invited some trusted friends into the process. If this was truly an invitation from God to take a small step toward deepening our practice of hospitality, we were open to God confirming this through others. We invited three of our friends from our church community to come and sit with our family. We made sure that each of our kids had an opportunity to have their voices heard. Our friends spent about ninety minutes asking each of us some questions and giving us all an opportunity to respond. Everyone got to voice their desires and their hesitations and the ways they were sensing God's leading. We got to hear our youngest grieve that she would need to share her oldest sister's last year at home with another person. And this opened up an even bigger process of listening as we learned that she was already grieving the fact that her older sister would leave for college in a year. Lots of tears! And many conversations about this topic have happened since then. She was able to name this pre-grieving during our discernment process simply because we created space for everyone to do some deeper listening.

In the end we decided to host Ellie for her senior year. We felt settled that this was something that God was inviting us into—to practice hospitality at a deeper level as a family. There were several times throughout those ten months that challenges came up—of course they did! Adding someone into the mix of any family will create ample opportunity for new challenges to emerge. But because we did all the discernment work on the frontside, we could rest in the fact that this was not a decision we entered lightly. Even when the everyday challenges emerged, we never doubted that we had made the right decision.

Consenting to the Constraints of One Another

Decisions like the one I just shared may not feel like big ones requiring all these steps of discernment. But for our kids—three teenagers and one in grade school—it felt like a big decision. There are likely decisions being made in church communities that feel like substantial ones for some while barely registering for others. We all have our own sense of what constitutes big or small. We all bring our own histories and stories into this process. Even if decisions don't appear to require all these steps, why not use the opportunity to practice listening carefully to one another? *Why does this decision feel big for you? What's at stake for you? For the community? What is being stirred up in you as we face this decision together?*

What is lost in opening up the process other than time?

Of course, there are times when quick decisions need to be made. There are moments in leadership when it's the job of a leader to make decisions *for* the group rather than *with* the group. But if it's possible to slow down and practice discernment, there are so many moments for community building and loving one another through the process. One of the friends we invited into the discernment process about hosting Ellie shared with us afterward that it touched something deep inside her, watching how each family member was given a voice in a decision that would impact the family. She noted how empowered even our youngest (ten years old at the time) felt to give input into the decision process. She shared that it touched something in her own story and helped her gain access to some pain she was carrying for not having been given a voice in an important situation in her life. What she noticed was the commitment to *mutuality.*

Mutuality is the capacity to recognize that our life is lived in relation to other lives. We are intertwined. Our needs and desires often stand in contradiction to the needs and desires of others. But even when this is so, a community can commit to being sustained by negotiation and by the practice of giving and receiving that a commitment to mutuality requires.

There are very real and natural constraints found within our relationships. Unless we live alone, work alone, and have no neighbors, we probably will have plenty of opportunities to notice how others' needs and desires will present constraints on our life. We basically have two options: we can oppose the constraints that others' wishes would impose on us or we can consent to them as an opportunity to learn how to love. This was the struggle I faced when the idea of hosting another person in our home for ten months presented itself. My first instinct was, "No way!" And I probably could have shut the conversation down. In fact, there is a version of myself from years ago that would have done this very thing. But the commitment to mutuality and to consenting to the possibility that community requires me to be open to not getting my way—even when I have the *power* to make it my way.

These little constraints are more or less inconsequential to our life. In the end, they can become small ascetic training opportunities that allow us to pay attention to how attached we are to getting our own way. *What unhealed passions are at work in this circumstance? Why am I so angry about this? Where is all this resistance coming from?*

We learn, through paying attention, that in the end, we actually don't need to get our own way. There has been a long season in our house, for example, where simply choosing a restaurant creates ample room for everyone to learn the delicate art of both saying out loud what they want, while almost never actually getting what they want. With six people with differing tastes and appetites, we always have some training in paying attention to the strength of our own will available in these moments. You don't have to call this asceticism if you don't want to—but it's sometimes an emotional workout. This has often provided opportunity for practicing faults and affirmations later in the week!

Spend a few days noticing how many opportunities are available for you to practice *consenting* to the inconsequential constraints on your life that naturally come up in your relationships. Write them down and notice how you are interacting with these constraints.

Consciously consenting to these microconstraints helps us learn mutuality in our daily lives with others. But what does this have to do with the practice of discernment in community? It will be difficult to allow others to offer input into our life that could result in some consequential changes if we are not already paying attention to the natural, everyday constraints of others' impact on our lives in ways that are inconsequential. We need small ways of practicing *consent* to the constraints that other's lives place on us before we are able to learn how to consent to the larger constraints that others might put on us—particularly when it comes to some of the major decisions of our lives. If we can start with a light lift—consenting to the inconveniences that are wrapped up in community—then we might be able to work our way up to a heavier lift: allowing others to speak into our lives about our decisions and what they see God shaping us toward. Discernment is about the willingness to be in a relationship of mutuality *within* the most important areas of our lives.

The practice of discernment in community may be the most difficult of any of the practices that we've leaned into so far because it is the one that takes the longest to materialize. It is also the practice that most relies on others, and it carries with it the highest stakes.

Growing Toward the Practice of Discernment in Community

The practice of discernment within community is difficult because it requires a whole *way of life* among multiple people. Here is the process of forming this kind of community.

First, commit to becoming a person who is learning to listen carefully to the presence of God in your own life. There are some skills that we can practice individually to learn to pay deeper attention to the inner movements of the Holy Spirit. The Holy Spirit is guiding each individual Christian from within. The tools the Spirit uses to speak to the individual are primarily the word of God spoken through the Scriptures, through the community of believers surrounding the individual, and through the individual's own *sense* of God's leading and guiding through their thoughts and emotions. The Holy Spirit is God inside of us coming alongside—from the Greek *parakletos*—to guide us. But if you've ever tried to navigate a difficult decision or considered walking into something new or struggled to stay put in something that has become difficult, you know that getting clarity in the midst of competing thoughts and emotions can be quite challenging. Remember, the unhealed passions begin in the thoughts and are often expressed in the emotions (or the "affections" as they used to be called). Thoughts and emotions are both the seedbed of nearly everything that goes wrong in our life. This is why many in the Western Christian tradition (particularly American evangelicalism) have taught that emotions cannot be trusted and we must "take every thought captive" (2 Cor 10:5). It's a little more complex than this.

It's true, most of the passions begin in the thoughts and get expressed in and through the emotions (wrath, envy, vainglory, etc.). But the gift of the Holy Spirit living inside of us means that God is also active in our thoughts and emotions. If these are the places where our flesh and the enemy are manipulating us toward error, what makes us think that these are not also the places where God himself would show up with his presence to heal all that is not well? God is there with the kindness and generosity of his own self. We simply need to pay attention and learn to discern between the invitation of God and everything else. As Jules Toner writes, "The direct promptings of the Holy Spirit as

Paraclete arise within our complex, flowing, conscious life that is hidden from all but God and self; and they have to be distinguished from our own spontaneous impulses (egoistic or generous) and from the promptings of our environment (good or bad), or the evil spirit."[8]

This process of discernment within the tradition we're drawing from is called the "discernment of spirits." It comes to us primarily from the *Spiritual Exercises* of Saint Ignatius of Loyola, though these principles stretch all the way back to the desert fathers. It was Saint Ignatius who gave us *rules* for discernment—a road map of being attentive to oneself. He developed the spiritual exercises for ordinary artisans, moms, and students as much as for monks and priests. It's a retreat for normal people who desire to make an extraordinary commitment to Jesus. Within these exercises he gave instructions to those leading others through them—spiritual directors—for how to help us more deeply notice those inner moments.

The best thing you can do to learn the discernment of these inner movements of thoughts and emotions and to take action in response to what you have learned is to journey through the spiritual exercises with a spiritual director who is trained to guide you through them.[9]

Second, invite others into the deepest movements in your spiritual life through spiritual friendship and spiritual direction. The tradition of spiritual direction, which goes all the way back to the early church fathers and mothers, is now broadly accepted within many churches in North America. The simplest way of describing spiritual direction is the help one person gives another in their spiritual growth and development. It's also been described as the divine art of healing another's wounds.

Opening up our life to another in a formal relationship like spiritual direction or a more informal one in spiritual friendship, which also features in the monastic tradition, nurtures the humility required for discernment. It's a great help having another set of ears to help us hear. It's a way of putting into practice the belief that we cannot do this alone. A Cistercian monk and abbot in the twelfth century, Aelred of Rievaulx, said that "Friendship is a step toward the love and knowledge of God. In friendship indeed, there is nothing dishonest, nothing feigned, nothing pretended."[10]

As we grow into the practice of discernment we frequently need people who will be able to reflect back to us and listen to us say out loud our tentative conclusions about what God might be doing in us. There are times when we reach conclusions that others are able to immediately confirm because they too see this in us. Other times we need others to reflect back to us how they see what's happening in us differently. Without the deep spiritual friendships in my life over the past decade, the unhealed passions in me could have led me down some very different paths. I have had two spiritual directors over the past fifteen years. These men have prayed with me and for me and have reflected back to me difficult things as well as glorious things that I could not see about my life and the work that God was doing in me.

Finding spiritual friendship is challenging. Our lives are busy. Most people in our society are primarily oriented toward work and family. The kind of spiritual friendship that can hold some of our deepest and most intimate thoughts and our hopes for the ongoing healing work of God in our lives requires a tremendous amount of discipline and investment—but it might bring us to freedom. In speaking of a long-term spiritual friendship, Aelred of Rievaulx writes of his friend:

He brought me peace in trouble; he calmed my anger. Whatever unpleasantness occurred, I referred to him, so that whatever I could not endure alone I could endure shoulder to shoulder with him. Was that not like the first fruits of bliss, so *to love and* so *to be loved*, to help and to be helped, and from the sweetness of brotherly love to fly aloft toward that higher place in the splendor of divine love, or from the ladder of charity now to soar to the embrace of Christ himself, or, now descending to the love of one's neighbor, there sweetly to rest?

A friendship that points us to the love of Christ and neighbor is one that takes intentionality. My hope is that the people you have been reading this book with, given all the deeper conversations you've been having, might become good candidates for deepening spiritual friendship together.

Third, practice formal group discernment as needed. As we grow in personal discernment and allow a small circle of spiritual friends into our discernment of God's work in our lives, we can also begin to practice more formal modes of discernment in community. If you are part of a staff or leadership team at your church (or perhaps you *are* the leader) there will be endless opportunities, once the team is oriented to the necessity of this practice, to open up key decisions to a process of discernment. There are some practical steps for formal and semiformal practices of discernment for pastors, small groups, and families at the end of this chapter.

The Freedom to Trust

The opposite of humility is pride. Pride sees all situations of discernment—the decisions of our life, the possibility that God is doing something in us—through one perspective: our own eyes. Pride trusts in our own ability to navigate both our outer world (decisions) and inner world (thoughts and emotions). Even when we do consider letting others into our life, pride often immediately assigns less importance to the input of others when compared to our own input. We do this mostly without even being aware of it.

But humility begins to know and live into the reality that our ability to see clearly has been compromised by an array of un-healed passions—we all are motivated by self-protection, the desire for love from others, and having some sense of control in the world. And all of these will hinder our ability to see clearly and respond courageously to the invitations that the gospel offers us. Throughout the whole Christian tradition pride has always been seen as the greatest and most formidable of the passions. Pride simply will not allow us to trust in God.

Pride leads us to self-protection where we might hide and hold back information that could be helpful in decisions that we need to make. We don't always do this on purpose—the subconscious is very strong. But we do not know how to bring everything to bear upon a decision because we do not have the people around us who can bear it with us. The only way we can get to some things in our life is with the help of others. We do not have these people around us because we have kept them at a distance. And so some helpful information in our soul lies hidden simply because we do not have eyes to see it. The practice of inviting others to speak into our lives acts against our desire for self-protection.

In our desire to be loved, pride causes us to attempt to earn love by our own doing. We think that if we can be good enough and tell the right stories about our life, then all will be well. We find ourselves telling the truth only halfway. We tell the stories that cast us in the brightest of lights. Again, we can't quite see this about ourselves—even half of the time. But these stories also obscure the very beautiful things that are happening in our life in the most vulnerable places. We cannot get to them, nor can we let them shape our life decisions because we haven't yet learned that those places we want to hide are the very places where God is patiently waiting for us.

Or we work too hard for the approval of others. When others reach out to us to care for us, pride says, "I'm fine." Even when there is a part of us that knows that we are not fine, we ignore our needs because we think not having needs will win the approval of others. Practicing discernment in community opens us up to the curiosity of others and allows them to see the flaws in our thinking and the depth of emotions that cause us to remain attached to things in ways that are harmful.

Our desire to feel in control of some part of our world skews our view of what God may or may not be doing in us. We come to believe that our life is solely our responsibility. *I have control of my life. This life is my responsibility and mine alone!* And in some ways, it is. But this is only partly true. We assume that our responsibility for our life means that we have to carry ourselves and all the burdens that come with being in the world. We think we cannot be carried by others. Practicing discernment in community gives others the imagination to help bear the burdens that we cannot carry alone—which is most of them.

Practicing discernment in community is a gift to others because it helps others imagine not needing to be in total control of their life. It helps them see that they too are worthy of love as they offer their presence to you. *If he is willing to ask for help in discerning these things in his life, maybe I can ask for help too.* Practicing discernment in community helps others see how beautiful it is when brothers and sisters dwell together in unity, even when they think differently about the direction of our ministry, our team, or our family.

When we open up the areas of life that we are navigating to others, or when we agree together to sort out this next decision with a commitment to mutuality, in the end we are not placing our trust in one another—we are placing our trust in God. We are entrusting our lives into the care of God. We are entrusting the life of others into the care of God.

PRACTICING
DISCERNMENT IN COMMUNITY

For Pastors and Leaders

This particular practice may be the one that most radically shifts the teams that we lead. It also has the capacity to transform the culture of our churches. It will also require us to lead from a place of commitment to slowly bend our teams toward deeper trust in one another.

Some next steps:

❖ Spend a season beginning to model what it looks like to allow the community of your team to offer constraints on your leadership. Ask for input more frequently. Choose to defer to the leadership of those below you on the org chart. You can do this while still articulating your thoughts and opinions that might differ from those of the ones who oversee a particular area of ministry. *Let's try it your way and see how it goes. I'll follow your lead.* This isn't necessarily practicing discernment together, but it begins to sow seeds of a discernment culture.

❖ When the next weighty decision comes along for you and your team, begin to cast a vision for what it might look like to slow the decision down and create a process of discernment.

❖ Read Ruth Haley Barton's *Pursuing God's Will Together* with your team or a portion of your team to give you some clear vision for this in your community.

❖ Notice what happens *within you* as you begin to shift your team's culture to a more communal discernment process. *Where are you experiencing resistance to letting others speak into the decisions for your community?*

❖ Do you have anything that you are personally navigating? A shift in your focus of vocation? Who in your life are you inviting into this process? Do you have people outside of your church community who can help you process in a safe way?

❖ Consider a long-term plan for training a team of leaders to help others within your community in their own discernment. This will be a long-term project. But can you imagine being able to offer to the people within your church a process that can help them discern together in community some of the larger decisions of their life? As you notice opportunities for group discernment emerge in the lives of those you shepherd, consider inviting people into a slower process of discernment.

❖ If you are not presently seeing a spiritual director, beginning a journey with a spiritual director will help you learn to listen carefully with ears toward discernment in your life.

For Small Groups

A small group of about five or six is best for this practice. If your group is larger than this, consider breaking into smaller groups. Inviting a large group of people to give input into a decision or speak freely about the work of God in one's life can feel overwhelming. Once you have a trusted group of people around you, use some of the questions below to begin to invite deeper input into one another's lives. Most of what needs to happen in a small group environment is preparation for discernment by creating a culture of deeper listening.

After everyone in the group has had an opportunity to share their story (one person per group meeting) spend some time as a group leaning into the following three questions. Again, this is creating a *culture* of discernment more than it is practicing discernment.

What in your life presently feels like it has the "fingerprints of God"?

How are you responding to what God is doing in your life?

How can we be present to you in your response to God?

Over time, hearing one another's stories and being present to one another's journeys with God will prepare you, as spiritual friends, to be present in moments when something needs to be discerned. With this culture of spiritual friendship as a foundation, the next time someone in your group has a bigger life decision to navigate—invite them to bring the decision to the group and help them listen carefully to what God might be inviting them toward. Help them notice the inner movements at work in their thoughts and emotions as they navigate the decision in prayer.

For Parents

I shared the story of hosting Ellie, an international student, as an example of how discernment can happen in the life of a family. Even with young kids you can begin nurturing an environment of discernment through inviting input into family decisions. Including your kids in simple decisions at a young age will create a culture of mutuality. Oftentimes as parents we think that our perspective will always be filled with the most wisdom. As kids get older, this is not always the case. Be open to the perspective of your children.

❖ Spend some time thinking and praying about what spiritual friendship might look like in your home. While we will always be our kids' parents, most of our relationship over time will be a kind of *spiritual friendship*. Learn to ask open-ended questions. Lead with curiosity about your kids' lives.

❖ Try to share openly about your own process of listening carefully to what God might be saying to you. As you make your adult decisions, bring your kids in on the process (appropriately). Maybe you are considering a new job. Or buying a new car. Include them in the process as best you can. Help them see that these kinds of decisions are full of sifting.

When I was deciding whether to write this book I talked with each of my kids about what it would cost me (margin, time, mental and emotional energy) above and beyond my normal work. At one point, one of my girls asked, "Dad, do you *want* to write this book?" And when I told her that I did, she replied, "Then I think you should write the book." It was a little boost. I needed to make the commitment. And I told her that her input was helpful to me.

❖ Look for opportunities to make decisions that will affect the whole family *as* a family. This doesn't mean that you even need consensus to move forward. But opening up the process will nurture some beautiful conversations.

FINAL WORD

WEEDS AND WHEAT

I n Matthew's Gospel, Jesus compares the kingdom of God to a person who sows good seed in a field. And then while he sleeps, someone else, an enemy, comes and sows weeds among the wheat. The weeds and the wheat grow up together, their roots intertwined. The temptation is to try to pull the weeds out. But at some point, for the very fact that they have grown up together, the weeds and the wheat grow side by side until they can be sorted out at harvest time. Better to let them grow together rather than risk losing the good things while trying to pull out the bad. In Jesus' parable the wheat represents the ones who embrace the kingdom and the weeds are the ones who have been sewn into the world by the enemy. The point of the story is that the Son of Man is responsible for the work of sorting at harvest time.

I have taken great comfort in this. God himself will sort out the weeds and the wheat in the world. And if God is willing to take responsibility for this task for all of creation, then most certainly he will also do the same for the weeds and the wheat that are growing within my own self. I'm often tempted to violently try to pull out the weeds—those that choke out the life of the Spirit's work. And then I remember that God is the primary worker in my field. And I open up my hands to him and offer a prayer of trust. And I know that for the rest of my life God will, in his love for me, feed and nurture the wheat and starve out the weeds.

As much as I believe that our work with God is one of participation, I also believe that Christ has done and is continuing to do the heavy lifting. The work of spiritual disciplines in the life of community reminds us that Christ is in us, compelling and fueling every bit of transformation by pouring God's love into our hearts through the Holy Spirit.

In all of this work of paying attention to and receiving the constraints in our life, the most important experience we can have is the experience of the love of God. Whatever is in the way of that experience, God is already at work to remove the barriers and the chains and the distractions.

And in this we can rest.

Solitude and silence helps us do this in the present moment. We have to face our experience of the world right now. And then we invite the Holy Spirit into that moment to speak and to pour out the love of God into our hearts.

Simplicity clears away external distractions and numbing techniques. We remove some of the comforts in our external world for short seasons and with regularity to simply be able *to see* what those comforts are comforting. What wound are those comforts tending? The practice of simplicity trains us away from fueling the desires leading us away from presence to God. We give up our attachments to the things of this world and ask God to fill in the gap left behind. And he does.

Marriage and celibacy are both containers where we learn how to give up our life, in various degrees, for the sake of another. We learn how to love.

Formational healing is our partnership with God's deep work of untangling our interior world and bringing healing through showing us that in the greatest places of our weakness, God is right there loving us. It is consenting to the reality that the treasure of God has been placed in fragile vessels—you and me.

Faults and affirmations helps us name what is true about ourselves and others. Something happens to us when we say these things out loud in the presence of others.

Discernment in community forms in us a willingness to recognize that we do not have everything we need, and we cannot see everything we need to see in order to make some decisions in our lives. We need others who are able to see what we cannot see.

An Invitation

If working your way through these constraints has stirred something of God's work in you, I invite you to lean into this work a little deeper. In the monastic tradition, both the rich and the poor would show up at a monastery door asking to be received into a life of community and into a lifetime of allowing God to sift the weeds and the wheat. We're building a global community in the tradition of the religious orders that have come before us. It is this tradition that has held fast to the centrality of the love of God, the constraints that do the work of clearing away the weeds, and the freedom that comes through the experience of God's love.

To take your next step on this journey visit www.orderofthe commonlife.org.

My Lord God,

I have no idea where I am going.

I do not see the road ahead of me.

I cannot know for certain where it will end.

nor do I really know myself,

and the fact that I think I am following your will

does not mean that I am actually doing so.

But I believe that the desire to please you

does in fact please you.

And I hope I have that desire in all that I am doing.

I hope that I will never do anything apart from that desire.

And I know that if I do this you will lead me by the right road,

though I may know nothing about it.

Therefore, will I trust you always though

I may seem to be lost and in the shadow of death.

I will not fear, for you are ever with me,

and you will never leave me to face my perils alone.[1]

GRATITUDES

I feel, in many ways, that I have been working on this book for more than a decade. Trying to capture the extent of gratitude on a few pages is impossible. The thing I am most grateful for in this season is the love I have found in friendship and collaboration in ministry.

My ecclesial home, for my entire adult life, has been the Vineyard. I walked into a Vineyard church in 1994 and encountered the love of God in a way that I am still trying to learn how to give away. My work with the Order of the Common Life (OCL), out of which this book has grown, has been stewarded within the care of leaders and friends within the Vineyard since 2012 (first under the greenhouse and partnership with Sustainable Faith, and in friendship and spiritual direction with Dave Nixon). I'm grateful for friends who have intentionally encouraged my life, my writing, and my vocation (Jay Pathak, John and Kara Kim, Adam Russell, Caleb Maskell, Ted Kim, Tyler Staton, Robb Morgan, Jeff Cannell, Michael Gatlin, Steve Summerell, Evan Howard). There are countless others who have prayed for me and spoken words directly to my heart.

My local church has been a gift. The Abbey Columbus is a contemplative Vineyard church in Columbus, Ohio. Our team has been so faithful to the work that God has entrusted to us. I'm grateful for Hannah Estabrook, Rachel General, and Heather Kristine for the labor of love that pastoring and caring for people through the pandemic has been. Thank you for persevering with me. Thank you for holding the story of my own formational healing journey during the year when the majority of this book was written. Thank you for building a community that can hold the *love of God* as the primary work that we steward. I love the way that God's presence has shown up for us.

I am deeply grateful for those on the journey with me toward reimagining "religious vocations" through the work of OCL. Brian Holmeier and Heather Kristine, both vowed members of OCL, have been helping me build something very beautiful over the last few years. Ted and Brittany Kim have both been a tremendous encouragement to me through years of me trying to find the courage to settle into what has felt like a peculiar assignment. I've leaned on John Kim and Caleb Maskell for wisdom and reassurance in moments when I've been confronted by my own weakness. JR Rozko, Todd Hunter, and Erick Stumberg are helping me imagine OCL extending outside my own ecclesial boundaries and into Bishop Hunter's Diocese of Churches for the Sake of Others (C4SO). I've worked out many of my thoughts in the context of conversations and cohorts with people walking through our formation process with OCL. Thank you for joining me in such vulnerable conversations about freedom and constraint.

Special thanks to InterVarsity Press for seeing the vision for this book, and to Al Hsu for helping to shape it and for thoughtful engagement in the editorial process. Wesley Hill was helpful in offering some feedback on the chapter on marriage and celibacy, and Geoff Holsclaw provided input in various places across several chapters.

It is impossible to express the gratitude I feel for my wife, Jaime, and our girls, Rayli, Talitha, Sadie, and Josephine. The joy that you all bring and the way that you have held space for God's transforming work in our family continues to be for me a vision of the slow and miraculous work of the Spirit through our life together.

God has made us rich in love.

NOTES

Introduction

[1] Roberta C. Bondi, *To Love as God Loves: Conversations with the Early Church* (Philadelphia: Fortress, 1987), 11.

[2] See https://brenebrown.com for many helpful books by Brené Brown.

[3] Chuck DeGroat, *When Narcissism Comes to Church: Healing Your Community from Emotional and Spiritual Abuse* (Downers Grove, IL: InterVarsity Press, 2020).

[4] For a thorough overview of how the written rule of life came to be, see Giorgio Agamben and Adam Kotsko, *The Highest Poverty: Monastic Rules and Form-of-Life* (Stanford, CA: Stanford University Press, 2013).

[5] Esther De Waal, *Seeking God* (Collegeville, MN: Liturgical, 2001), 18.

[6] Dallas Willard, *The Spirit of the Disciplines: Understanding How God Changes Lives* (San Francisco: Harper & Row, 1988), ix.

[7] Willard, *Spirit of the Disciplines*, xi.

[8] Willard, *Spirit of the Disciplines*, ix.

[9] The Order of the Common Life was originally the Order of Sustainable Faith. In 2020 we launched from underneath Sustainable Faith, which served as a wonderful greenhouse in those early years. The Order of the Common Life is ecclesially tied to Vineyard USA, though we work in a multitude of denominations and affiliations.

1. River, the Womb, and Hearth

[1] Hildegard von Bingen, *Scivias*, translated by Columba Hart and Jane Bishop (Mahwah, NJ: Paulist Press, 1990), 196.

[2] For a visual, Google "vividmaps changing river paths." See Zoltan Sylvester, "Rivers through Time, as Seen in Landsat Images," *Hindered Settling: Random Notes of a Skeptical Geologist* (blog), March 16, 2014, https://hinderedsettling.com/2014/03/16/rivers-through-time-as-seen-in-landsat-images.

[3] Father John Behr is one of the most important living theologians today. He bridges the gap between Eastern Orthodox theological traditions and the traditions of Western churches. Some of Fr. Behr's lectures are widely available on the internet. I commend them to you. He provides a rich theological underpinning for this thought experiment.

[4] "Abba Joseph," *Sayings of the Desert Fathers*, Orthodox Wiki, last edited May 8, 2020, https://orthodoxwiki.org/Sayings_of_the_Desert_Fathers#Abba_Joseph.

2. Freedom

[1] Thomas Merton, *Thomas Merton on the Twelve Steps of Humility* (Silver Spring, MD: Now You Know Media, 2012).

[2] Marlena Graves, *The Way Up Is Down: Becoming Yourself by Forgetting Yourself* (Downers Grove, IL: InterVarsity Press, 2020).

[3] Columba Stewart, "Evagrius Ponticus and the Eastern Monastic Tradition on the Intellect and the Passions," *Modern Theology* 27, no. 2 (April 2011): https://doi.org/10.1111/j.1468-0025.2010.01675.x.

[4] Roberta C. Bondi, *To Love as God Loves: Conversations with the Early Church* (Philadelphia: Fortress, 1987), 57.

[5] John Chrysostom, *On Wealth and Poverty* (Crestwood, NY: St. Vladimir's Seminary Press, 1984).

[6] Gregory the Great, *The Book of Pastoral Rule* (Crestwood, NY: St. Vladimir's Seminary Press, 2007).

[7] M. S. Laird, *Into the Silent Land: A Guide to the Christian Practice of Contemplation* (Oxford, UK: Oxford University Press, 2006), 81.

[8] Drawn from themes in Dallas Willard, *The Spirit of the Disciplines: Understanding How God Changes Lives* (San Francisco: Harper & Row, 1988).

[9] Interview with the author, Columbus, OH, July 7, 2020.

[10] Basil, *On the Human Condition* (Crestwood, NY: St. Vladimir's Seminary Press, 2005), 37.

[11] Nonna Verna Harrison, *God's Many-Splendored Image: Theological Anthropology for Christian Formation* (Grand Rapids, MI: Baker Academic, 2010), 9.

[12] Augustine, *Confessions* (New York: Modern Library, 2018), 8-10.

[13] James K. A. Smith, *On the Road with Saint Augustine: A Real-World Spirituality for Restless Hearts* (Grand Rapids, MI: Brazos, 2019), 59-76.

[14] Jim Wilder and Dallas Willard, *Renovated: God, Dallas Willard & the Church That Transforms* (Colorado Springs: NavPress, 2020), 99.

3. Constraint

[1] Gerard Manley Hopkins, "As Kingfishers Catch Fire," in *Poems and Prose of Gerard Manley Hopkins* (Harmondsworth, Middlesex: Penguin, 1985), 51.

[2] Thomas Merton, *New Seeds of Contemplation* (New York: New Directions, 1972), 32.

[3] *Saint Gregory of Nyssa: Ascetical Works*, ed. Virginia Woods Callahan and Roy J. Deferrari (Washington, DC: Catholic University of America Press, 1999), 70.

[4] André Louf, *The Way of Humility* (Kalamazoo, MI: Cistercian, 2007), 12.

[5] Dallas Willard, *The Spirit of the Disciplines: Understanding How God Changes Lives* (San Francisco: Harper & Row, 1988), 166.

4. Practicing Constraint

[1] Jared Boyd, *Imaginative Prayer: A Yearlong Guide for Your Child's Spiritual Formation* (Downers Grove, IL: InterVarsity Press, 2017).

[2] John Cassian, *Conferences*, quoted in Thomas Merton, *Cassian and the Fathers: Initiation into the Monastic Tradition* (Kalamazoo, MI: Cistercian, 2005), 205.

[3] Oliver O'Donovan, *Common Objects of Love: Moral Reflection and the Shaping of Community: The 2001 Stob Lectures* (Grand Rapids, MI: Eerdmans, 2002).

5. Silence and Solitude

[1] Tish Harrison Warren, *Liturgy of the Ordinary: Sacred Practices in Everyday Life* (Downers Grove, IL: InterVarsity Press, 2016).

[2] *The Sayings of the Desert Fathers: The Alphabetical Collection*, trans. Benedicta Ward (Trappist, KY: Cistercian Publications, 1984), 8.

[3] Evagrius, *Talking Back: A Monastic Handbook for Combating Demons* (Trappist, KY: Cistercian, 2009), 1-40.

[4] John Mark Comer, *Live No Lies: Recognize and Resist the Three Enemies That Sabotage Your Peace* (Colorado Springs, CO: WaterBrook, 2021).

[5] *John Cassian: Conferences*, trans. Colm Luibheid, Classics of Western Spirituality (New York: Paulist, 1985), 51.

[6] Some of the shift in this strategy is a result of learning about some new modalities within the therapeutic world, specifically Richards Swartz's work on internal family systems and "parts-work." See *No Bad Parts: Healing Trauma and Restoring Wholeness with the Internal Family Systems Model* (Louisville: Sounds True, 2021).

[7] The Ignatian tradition calls this process the "discernment of spirits." See Timothy Gallaugher, *The Discernment of Spirits: An Ignatian Guide for Everyday Living* (New York: Crossroad, 2005).

[8] I am almost certain I first heard this from one of the recordings of Thomas Merton's lectures to his novitiates at the Abbey of Gethsemeni.

[9] John Cassian, *Conferences* 9.18. Merton works his way through the Latin word by word until he comes to this translation.

[10] Thomas Merton, *The Contemplative Way* (Silver Spring, MD: Now You Know Media, 2016).

[11] Thomas Merton, *The Wisdom of the Desert: Sayings from the Desert Fathers of the Fourth Century* (New York: New Directions, 1970), 8.

[12] Dallas Willard, *Life Without Lack: Living in the Fullness of Psalm 23* (Nashville: Thomas Nelson, 2018), xviii.

6. Simplicity

[1] See www.thelightphone.com.

[2] Basil and Nona Verna Harrison, *On the Human Condition* (Crestwood, NY: St. Vladimir's Seminary Press, 2005), 93-105.

[3] Basil, *On the Human Condition*, 98.

[4] One example is our use of technology. For a helpful resource, see Andy Crouch, *The Tech-Wise Family: Everyday Steps for Putting Technology in Its Proper Place* (Grand Rapids, MI: Baker, 2017).

[5] For more on this topic see Jim Wilder and Dallas Willard, *Renovated: God, Dallas Willard & The Church That Transforms* (Colorado Springs, CO: NavPress, 2020).

[6] Joan Chittister, *Illuminated Life: Monastic Wisdom for Seekers of Light* (New York: Orbis, 2010), 100.

[7] It's always good to consult a doctor before fasting longer than twenty-four hours.

[8] This cohort was part of our introductory discernment process for the Order of the Common Life where we spend six months talking through our rule of life.

[9] Our own rule of life in the Order of the Common Life offers an invitation toward simplicity of clothing, though there is no commitment to specific clothing.

[10] John Cassian, *Institutes* 1.1, www.newadvent.org/fathers/350701.htm

[11] Giorgio Agamben and Adam Kotsko, *The Highest Poverty: Monastic Rules and Form-of-Life* (Stanford, CA: Stanford University Press, 2014), 14.

[12] Ananya Bali, "Modern Slavery in Fast Fashion Brands," *Fashion & Law Journal*, October 3, 2021, https://fashionlawjournal.com/modern-slavery-in-fast-fashion-brands/.

[13] Ignatius of Loyola, *Ignatius of Loyola: The Spiritual Exercises and Selected Works*, ed. George E. Ganss (New York: Paulist Press, 1991), 130.

[14] Basil and C. Paul Schroeder, *On Social Justice: St. Basil the Great* (Crestwood, NY: St. Vladimir's Seminary Press, 2009), 23.

[15] Stewart, Columba, "The Greening of Asceticism," *The Way* 31, no. 4 (October 1991): 303-12.

7. Marriage and Celibacy

[1] Mike Cosper and Russell Moore, *The Rise and Fall of Mars Hill*, podcast audio, Season 1, ep. 18, 2022.

[2] See Rachel Joy Welcher, *Talking Back to Purity Culture: Rediscovering Faithful Christian Sexuality* (Downers Grove, IL: InterVarsity Press, 2020).

[3] Wesley Hill and Karen Keen, Streckert Lecture on Christianity, Sexuality, and Gender, Wheaton College, April 5, 2022.

[4] The Order of the Common Life offers a pathway of discernment of a vocation to lifelong celibacy.

[5] Ronald Rolheiser, *Sacred Fire: A Vision for a Deeper Human and Christian Maturity* (New York: Doubleday, 2017), 19.

[6] Christopher A. Hall, *Living Wisely with the Church Fathers* (Downers Grove, IL: InterVarsity Press, 2017), 149.

[7] Gerald Hiestand and Todd A. Wilson, *Beauty, Order, and Mystery: A Christian Vision of Human Sexuality* (Downers Grove, IL: InterVarsity Press, 2017), 73.

[8] See Tish Warren Harrison, "I Married the Wrong Person and I'm So Glad I Did," *New York Times*, June 6, 2022, www.nytimes.com/2022/06/05/opinion/marriage-satisfaction-love.html.

[9] Stanley Hauerwas, "Sex and Politics: Bertrand Russell and 'Human Sexuality,'" *Christian Century*, April 18, 1978, 417-22, www.religion-online.org/article/sex-and-politics-bertrand-russell-and-human-sexuality/.

[10] Hall, *Living Wisely*, 158.

[11] There are several men and women who are navigating and leading this conversation. I am most familiar with the work of Episcopal priest and professor of New Testament Wesley Hill, as well as David Bennet, who wrote *A War of Loves: The Unexpected Story of a Gay Activist Discovering Jesus* (Grand Rapids, MI: Zondervan, 2018).

[12] For more information about a noncoercive approach to discernment around LGBTQ+ conversations, see https://postureshift.com.

[13] For an up-to-date overview of two perspectives, see Wesley Hill and Karen Keen's Streckert Lecture, www.youtube.com/watch?v=KWPx7jJy094.

[14] I'm grateful for ongoing conversation with my friend and colleague Heather Kristine, OCL. She has broadened my understanding of celibacy as a calling as I have journeyed with her.

[15] Personal email correspondence between Karen Keen and Wesley Hill, quotation posted at https://wesleyhill.tumblr.com/post/59406860622/when-christians-sell-books-and-preach-sermons.

[16] Rolheiser, *Sacred Fire*, 69.

[17] Roberta C. Bondi, *To Love as God Loves* (Philadelphia: Fortress, 1987), 25.

8. Formational Healing

[1] I agree with Chuck DeGroat, who notes that our categories for psychological and mental health struggles and the way we talk about the spiritual forces of evil often overlap. See his *Wholeheartedness: Busyness, Exhaustion, and Healing the Divided Self* (Grand Rapids, MI: Eerdmans, 2016).

[2] Gregory of Nyssa and Catharine P. Roth, *The Soul and the Resurrection* (Crestwood, NY: St. Vladimir's Seminary Press, 1993), 8.

[3] Gregory of Nyssa, *On the Soul and the Resurrection*, 84.

[4] For a wonderful account of what it means to walk through this process in the midst of ongoing pain and suffering see K. J. Ramsey, *This Too Shall Last: Finding Grace When Suffering Lingers* (Grand Rapids, MI: Zondervan, 2020).

9. Faults and Affirmations

[1] C. S. Lewis, *The Weight of Glory and Other Addresses* (New York: Macmillan, 1980), 18.

[2] For a deeper dive into this idea see David G. Benner, *The Gift of Being Yourself: The Sacred Call to Self-Discovery* (Downers Grove, IL: InterVarsity Press, 2004).

[3] For an overview of the false-self tradition see M. Basil Pennington, *True Self/False Self: Unmasking the Spirit Within* (New York: Crossroad, 2000).

[4] Thomas Merton, www.learn25.com/product/monastic-spirituality-the-quest-for -peace-html/.

[5] Augustine, *Confessions* (New York: Modern Library, 2018), 3-6, 11.

[6] Bernard, *The Steps of Humility and Pride* (Kalamazoo, MI: Cistercian Publications, 1989), 20.

[7] Rumer Godden, *In This House of Brede* (New York: Viking, 1969), 171. I am grateful for my friend Evan Howard who pointed me to this section of Godden's novel and who has given us the framework for the practice of faults and affirmations. In our first Rule of Life (2014) Evan wrote an essay on faults and affirmations, which has guided our practice within OCL as well as within my own family.

[8] Jacques Philippe, *Interior Freedom* (New York: Scepter, 2007), 38.

[9] Augustine, *Confessions* 10.5.7, 282-83.

[10] Michael Casey, *A Guide to Living in the Truth: Saint Benedict's Teaching on Humility* (Liguori, MO: Liguori/Triumph, 2006).

[11] Thomas Merton, *The Wisdom of the Desert: Sayings from the Desert Fathers of the Fourth Century* (New York: New Directions, 1970), 40.

10. Discernment in Community

[1] *The Rule of St. Benedict*, ed. Timothy Fry (New York: Vintage, 1998), 8.

[2] Aquinata Böckmann, *A Listening Community: A Commentary on the Prologue and Chapters 1-3 of Benedict's Rule* (Collegeville, MN: Liturgical, 2015), 85.

[3] *The Rule of St. Benedict*, 8.

[4] Michael Casey, *A Guide to Living in the Truth: Saint Benedict's Teaching on Humility* (Liguori, MO: Liguori/Triumph, 2006), 57.

[5] Ruth Haley Barton, *Pursuing God's Will Together: A Discernment Practice of Leadership Groups* (Downers Grove, IL: InterVarsity Press, 2012), 10.

[6] Hold Rom 8:3-3, Gal 6:2, and Mt 5:1; 7-20 together in meditation and prayer. You will see that the law was always meant to lead us toward love and bearing the burdens of one another in community.

[7] For additional resources see Barton, *Pursuing God's Will Together*; Thomas H. Green, *Weeds among the Wheat: Discernment: Where Prayer & Action Meet* (Notre Dame, IN: Ave Maria, 1984); Elizabeth Liebert, *The Soul of Discernment: A Spiritual Practice for Communities and Institutions* (Louisville, KY: Westminster John Knox, 2015); Steve Macchia, *The Discerning Life: An Invitation to Notice God in Everything* (Grand Rapids, MI: Zondervan, 2022).

[8] Jules J. Toner, *Discerning God's Will: Ignatius of Loyola's Teaching on Christian Decision Making* (Saint Louis, MO: Institute of Jesuit Sources, 1991), 3.